Earth Angels

Written By: Gwen Michalek

Illustrated By: Jill Emerson

Edited by: Jill Emerson

Ginger Nordstrom

www.earthangelsbook.com

Email: abbacojoy@aol.com

Contents

Part 1

Part 2

Part 3

Part 4

Dedication

**This book is dedicated
to the "Earth Angels" of the world.**

Definition of an *earth angel*: *a messenger who inhabits the earth and works for God. (Could this be you?)*

You as an *earth angel* must now have faith the Lord will show you what you are called to do. For there are many chosen souls who are being called to serve in these times. We pray this book will be a source of inspiration for all. Go forward now with confidence KNOWING our Father will provide you with all you need to succeed for He has formed a covenant with you!

May the Lord bless and keep you all,

Love,

Wendy and Jillian

Acknowledgement

Jillian and I wish to give special thanks to Joseph Girzone for his support of Earth Angels. As a renowned author of the infamous Joshua Books we are indeed humbled by his enthusiastic response to our book. He can never know how often we have thought about him over the years, as he truly exemplifies the teachings of Jesus. We pray someday we can meet this man who has touched the hearts of so many.

We would also like to thank Father Bob who for many years supported Jillian and I in our spiritual adventures with ABBA and Company; most recently of which was the enthusiastic response to the unedited version of Earth Angels.

A heartfelt thanks goes to my sister and friend Ginger Nordstrom for her strategic suggestions, editing and invaluable help in bringing our book to completion! Her constructive input and enthusiasm helped to put the finishing touches on Earth Angels.

Thank you to Donna Kelly for her suggestions and editing of the earlier manuscript, as well as a thank you to Marla and Jeannie whose friendship and support has meant so much to the two of us on this journey.

We give special thanks to Jillian's mother, MaryKay, and grandmother, Catherine, who, through their example and teachings, helped us to undertand our journey from a spiritual nature. They have taught us the importance of faith and family and to always stand up for what is right, even if it is not popular! They are in heaven now and still guiding us along with Dick's mother, Doris.

Finally to our guys, Dick and Tom, we thank you both for your love and patience throughout this journey.

Love,

Wendy

Introduction

*"So, here goes, my little one. This is of the Divine.
Earth angels now have a clear understanding of what
is the reality and what is but an illusion. They fully
comprehend and understand these are the times earth
angels were destined for. Now it is up to each and every
one of you to listen to the stirrings which come from the
center of your being. You must believe nothing that is of
Me is a coincidence in these days. Each of you has a role
to fulfill and for each of you it will manifest in different
ways and circumstances. Yet, those who are earth
angels will understand these words are of Me and they
are to be shared with others. In reading these words
you will see the Greatest Plan of all time unfold before
your very eyes. You will be assured there are those of
you who are being gathered for these times and now
it is time to unite. These words will indeed prompt the
longings of your soul and remind each and every one
of My children of that which they are called to do and
be. They will assure each of you of that which you have
come from and of that which you will return to. Let these
words then bring you peace and solace in the days and
weeks to come. For these words will see you through
many difficult times ahead. Know then that I am always
there for each of you. Do not covet one another's gifts
but rather lift your hearts to the heavens above knowing*

that I and my host of angels are there for all of you now as never before. TRUST in the Divine with all of your heart, with all of your being, and each of you will indeed accomplish that which you have been called to do. Whenever two or more are gathered in My name they shall do good works as they are protected by that which is of the Divine and therefore no adversity shall keep them from that which is of our heavenly Father. I will not fail you and so it is I have formed a covenant with thee."

Divine Mercy Prayer

Lord grant that my eyes will see today what You would have them see. Let our minds be of one accord. Let the words that I speak be only the words that You would have me say. Let our hearts be united as one. I pray for a double anointing of the Holy Spirit to carry through my tasks today.

-ABBA and Company

Prologue

It has been well over twenty years since Jesus had shared with Wendy and Jillian they would be writing about the "Greatest Plan" on earth. It was at this time Jesus told Wendy she was a writer.

When the time was right they would remember all He had shared with them as though it had transpired yesterday. Now, more than two decades later, they knew without a shadow of a doubt these were the times they had been sent here for. These were the times that all they had been taught would be put into practice!

If Wendy and Jillian had known then what they know now they would have been totally overwhelmed, and that would be putting it mildly! Never in their wildest imaginations could they have comprehended the magnitude of the work they would be called to do.

Now, as they were preparing the final draft of the Earth Angels book, Jesus is appealing to all of His children to come to Him in the Holy sanctuaries of their beings. This is where all will seek the truth! This is where all will find shelter in the days and weeks ahead! Jesus was now implementing the stages of His plan in the final battle between good and evil on earth.

Wendy and Jillian prayed with all of their beings they had written the words exactly as Jesus had instructed them to do. They understood they had been sent to teach all how to commune with their Heavenly Father. It would be through this soulful connection one would find the answers they seek. Man must now trust they are being guided as soon the Lord would be revealing much to all. Soon, very soon, the Holy Spirit would be descending upon all of mankind.

"Tell them I am coming my daughters! I am making Myself known and soon each will need to make a choice. My Holy Spirit resides in all who accept this truth! I am connecting an invisible thread now amongst My children. This thread cannot be broken as I have formed a covenant with Thee!"

Part I

Part I

Chapter 1

The Beginning: The Great Plan

Our story begins in our Father's heavenly kingdom...

"The secret to living is in the giving," thought Wendy. "Just remember the secret to living is in the giving." Wendy could not even count how many times she had heard the Angel of Joy utter these final words, as she watched her beloved souls depart on their journey. For some, this was a journey that had been taken numerous times; too many times, as far as Wendy was concerned. There were too many souls who were just not getting it. If the truth be known there were those in the kingdom who felt time was running out. There were in fact, countless souls who had to make the same trip over and over again.

Wendy knew if it were up to her she would have very different words to say. Why, she would let them know in no uncertain terms this was their last chance. If they didn't get it right this time there would be no more chances. Yes, that is how she would do it if it were up to her.

Of course, Wendy knew this was precisely why she was not in charge of teaching the many souls intended for earth *The Art of Joy-filled Living.* In truth, it was not at all unusual for souls to return to earth many times in order to obtain the state of enlightenment desired. Although no soul was ever forced to return most desired to do so. Wendy knew it was only natural for a soul to return a few times, yet she felt far too many were not paying attention. Of course, she herself had never actually experienced life as a human and so it was difficult for her to fully understand. The Angel of Joy reminded Wendy of this important fact on more than one occasion. It was not that Wendy did not have compassion for these precious souls, as Wendy had been the guardian of many humans over the ages. It was just that Wendy did not have as much patience as Joy.

One must understand angels are created for the express purpose of serving our heavenly Father. Because they have been created for this specific purpose, they only desire to do what the Father asks. They exist to serve Him and Him only and as a result only desire to do what is in their Father's will.

Angels have not been given the so called "gift of free will". As a matter of fact, most angels do not think of free will as a gift at all. Wendy and the Angel of Joy had talked about this on many occasions over the years. Wendy felt it would have been much easier if Jesus hadn't given this free will to humans or at least given it in limited doses. In fact, Wendy felt so strongly about this very same subject she recently submitted a written suggestion to the Father.

Wendy suggested humans should only be allowed to experience free will for a limited time. The length of time would be determined by the results obtained on each journey. Of course, she hadn't worked out the details, mind you. She would leave the details up to Jesus as she didn't want to overstep her boundaries.

When Wendy shared her idea of limited free will for humans with her sister Jillian she was not prepared for the response she received. Usually she and Jillian saw eye to eye on everything. That is why she was not prepared for the peals of laughter that resonated from the center of Jillian's being. An angel's laughter resembles a tinkling bell. When an angel is truly tickled the sound of laughter can be heard throughout the kingdom. Wendy could remember the precise moment she shared this unique idea with Jillian.

When they were not on assignment or teaching the cherubs, Wendy and Jillian could be found drifting along the shoreline. Spreading their wings on top of the azure waters, they would float for hours on end. To any passerby this would be a most majestic sight indeed, as an angel's wingspan is well over twelve feet at its fullest capacity. Many times, using their wings as a head rest, they would be content to drift in silence; on other occasions they would talk about their recent assignments.

As guardian angels of humans they always had many stories to tell. They would share their frustrations as well as that which brought them joy. Jillian was most distressed on this particular day. On her last assignment she did not understand what it was she was supposed to accomplish.

Jillian 2012

If she hadn't been taken off of this assignment perhaps things would be different. It was this very potential for interference which caused St. Michael to replace Jillian with another guardian. Guardians were never allowed to interfere with the will of their assigned human. This could be most frustrating for guardians as they were not allowed to prohibit any of the choices their human would make. As guardians, they could only watch over their charge as they experienced the effects of the choices they made. Because of free will, many choices were made by humans which kept them from connecting with their soul and thus they could not discover their mission in life.

This could be most disconcerting for a guardian, especially when it involved a soul that had been recycled time and time again. This is when a guardian angel is most tempted to do the unforgivable, to interfere in the will of a human. The first rule in being a guardian of humans is to never interfere during this process. Human beings must be free to make their own choices. A guardian can only stand by to guide their charge once the choice has been made which could be very frustrating for the guardian angel.

One must understand there are no mistakes as far as Jesus is concerned. The purpose of life is to learn. Mistakes, as humans call them, are simply a part of their soul's development, part of their life's lesson plan. Although angels are aware of this fact, these lesson plans can be most painful to observe. There is a saying amongst the guardians, "No pain, No gain". Though all guardians understand sorrow is a necessary part of life's experience it is most difficult to watch. Once a lesson is learned humans are expected to share their lessons with others; this is also a part of the life process. Jesus says, ***"Mistakes allow you to practice those things which once learned enable you to share your newfound wisdom with others."*** However, too many souls do not share what they have learned and even when some do there are many who choose not to listen. So, as you can see, being a guardian of humans can be most frustrating indeed.

"I tell you, Jillian" exclaimed Wendy, "Jesus needs to draw the line with this free will thing! You and I both know that many souls are in jeopardy. I don't know about you, but I am tired of seeing the same souls go back time and time again. If it weren't for free will they would know what is important. They would know what matters. Don't they understand they are holding everything up? How can they ignore their souls so? It seems to be getting worse instead of better!"

"I know, Wendy," replied Jillian. "However, Jesus wants all souls to be able to choose their own particular lesson plan. You know He has faith they will eventually come to understand that which is the heart of the matter, and will come to know what is the key to life. All souls long to accomplish their mission, yet many become far too distracted. They are lured by the things of the world and do not listen to what comes from the center of their being. Alas, that is why so many souls make so many trips."

"Well, that is precisely why I put a suggestion in the elders' golden box," responded Wendy, "I think certain souls should not be allowed to make choices. They should be deprived of the gift of free will! I think giving free will to some humans has the same effect as when the cherubs eat too much candy! Do you remember when little Peter snuck into the snack cupboard and got into the chocolate? Why, his perfect white feathers had a green tinge for days. I think free will for some humans has the same effect on their souls! It literally makes them sick!"

It was at this point Jillian began to laugh. Well, perhaps laugh is putting it mildly. In truth, the sound was more like a clanging of bells than the gentle tinkling of bells one generally hears from a feminine angel. Instead, the horrific sound exploding from Jillian sounded more like the clanging of a herd of

cows running at breakneck speed. Never had she heard
Jillian so close to hysteria. In fact, she was laughing so
hard her angelic wings were having difficulty staying
atop the waters as her body convulsed from the spasms
within.

"What is so funny?" Wendy exclaimed. It was of course difficult to be heard over the clanging. "I think it is a perfectly valid solution. Time is running out you know. It is time to do things differently. Will you stop it! You're getting me wet!" Wendy was becoming most indignant. She was not enjoying being the source of Jillian's entertainment.

It took quite awhile for Jillian to contain herself. In truth, she would have continued laughing had she not accidentally swallowed what seemed like a gallon of water when an unruly wave caught her by surprise. "Serves her right," Wendy thought, as she watched her sister gasp for air.

It was this very wave that was the sobering catalyst for Jillian. When she was finally able to contain herself, Jillian could see Wendy was not at all amused. In fact, upon closer observation one could see she was most put out.

"Oh Wendy, I am so sorry. I didn't realize you were actually serious. You and I both know free will is as necessary to human life as joy is to an angel. I can't believe you honestly put that in the suggestion box. You will be the laughing stock of the whole kingdom! Surely, you didn't really do that?"

These were the last words Wendy needed to hear from her sister. She herself had many doubts before she got up enough courage to actually submit her suggestion. Wendy knew how absurd it sounded, yet in her heart she felt something had to be done. If Jillian only realized the courage it had taken for Wendy to submit this most profound idea she would never have carried on so. She couldn't blame Jillian for her response, yet she wished Jillian had reacted differently.

"I realize this is the way it has always been done, Jillian. You and I both know how discouraged Jesus has become of late. I have also heard Satan is using more and more tools to capture souls. I was simply trying to help! I was responding to our Father's call. After all He did say in the last meeting He wanted all of us to be thinking of ways to help more souls succeed. At least I offered a suggestion!"

"I know Wendy and I'm sorry," Jillian responded. "It is just that I can't imagine Jesus ever agreeing to such a thing! You know how set He is on the gift of free will. It isn't free will that is the problem. The problem is, as I see it, the choices humans make as a result of this freedom. Jesus wants all of His children to come to Him by their own choice and out of love for our Father. On the other hand, I do agree it would be so much easier if many made the right choices in the beginning."

The Angel of Joy had been watching Wendy and Jillian from the shoreline for some time now. She had heard the tinkling, well rather clanging of bells resounding from afar. Intuitively, she knew it had to come from one of her beloved mentees. Wendy and Jillian were well known throughout the kingdom for their sense of humor and childlike antics and sure enough, as she suspected, there they were the two of them creating quite a stir. However, this time she noticed Wendy did look most indignant. It was Jillian who was creating all the ruckus. She could only imagine what had caused Jillian to burst forth with such resounding laughter.

In heaven angels are assigned to different positions. Humans of course are familiar with guardian angels and are even familiar with some of the Senior Angels such as St. Peter and St. Michael. These angels rank very highly in the heavenly realm. What most humans do not realize is there are specific angels who are in charge of various tasks. As the Angel of Joy's name depicts her primary function, in the heavens and on earth, is to teach all souls about joy.

To help further your understanding you must realize there are many angels who are responsible for other tasks as well. There is for example, the Angel of Peace, who as a matter of fact, has been working overtime for quite awhile now. This is apparent when one looks at the history in the world. The Angel of Joy was often called upon by Jesus to share her joy with the Angel of Peace, as this could be a most tiresome job. There are many other angels as well. Just to name a few there are: the Angel of Compassion, Angel of Hope, the Angel of Kindness and so on and so on. Each of these angels mentors many younger angels on their specific gifts. They teach others to become experts in their fields.

Wendy and Jillian had a natural zest for life and were often seen amongst the cherubs. Because of their child-like nature they were a favorite of the kingdom's younger population. When they weren't on assignment they were in charge of entertaining the cherubs. Perhaps, of all of their tasks this was the one both Wendy and Jillian enjoyed the most. To the Angel of Joy, Wendy and Jillian were simply cherubs in a grown angel's body. Oh, she loved them so. They brought so much joy to all of those around them. Because of their childlike behavior there were those in the kingdom who thought them naïve, if not foolish at times. Joy knew they were not naïve but simply a personification of innocence in its purest form. Many times they would come back from an earthly assignment crushed by what they had seen on earth. It was not that they did not know certain dire conditions existed, it was just they could not accept there were those who would do such horrible things. For this reason Joy was known to be overly protective of the two. She knew more than any of the others how fragile they truly were.

That is why when Jesus told her of the plan He was thinking about, Joy had become most alarmed. Usually, she could be counted on more than the others to support any new ideas their Father may have. This time she knew she would do all she could to discourage Him. Although, she knew His idea had merit, she would do all she could to keep Him from selecting Wendy or Jillian. In truth, it was Wendy who had drawn attention to herself by submitting that most ridiculous idea.

If only she would have talked to Joy about her suggestion. Joy would never have let it come to fruition and perhaps she wouldn't have to deal with this preposterous idea. The best she could hope for now was that the Counsel of Elders would find the Father's idea absurd as well as impossible. The probability of the latter, of course, was not realistic as through Jesus all things are possible.

What the Father had in mind was to send one, if not several of His angels to earth in human form. Since they had worked for Him in the past and had never experienced human life, Jesus thought they would succeed. Humans of angelic descent would not be as easily distracted. They would intuitively know they were meant to serve Him. This would be the beginning of a master plan if it worked. There were many attributes humans needed to acquire in order to achieve the desired state of enlightenment. First and foremost on the agenda was the understanding of joy and its importance to a soul's development. Joy had been listening to His every word. She could not fully concentrate, as she was too busy thinking about what she could do to put an end to this absurd idea. It was when Joy heard how soon Jesus wanted His plan to start that she was pulled to full attention.

"And so Joy, I was wondering whether you thought Wendy and Jillian were up to the task?" Jesus asked. *"They certainly are the personification of joy and I know either of them would be most willing to serve. I wouldn't want you to say anything at the moment as I need to meet with the elders first. But to tell you the truth Joy, I have been thinking about this for quite some time now and truly do feel it can work. What I would like from you now is to be thinking of what they would need in order to succeed on earth. I know this will not be an easy task, yet I am confident with the right training it can be done. I can see I have taken you by surprise, Joy.*

I am aware of how very fond you are of Wendy and Jillian. Yet, I tell you this will be quite an

accomplishment. There are still many details which will need to be worked out, therefore, do not worry Joy. There is much to be done before this shall come to fruition. I simply wanted to plant the seed with you now. I will be meeting with St. Michael and the others before anything concrete is decided upon. Go now, my cherub, and know all is well."

There was no way the Angel of Joy would say anything to her precious mentees of her recent visit with Jesus. She felt certain if either of them knew they were being considered for this most unique task they would not hesitate to accept, if not volunteer. Standing at the seashore watching the two of them now, Joy could not even begin to think of the heavenly kingdom without their childish antics. Wendy and Jillian were so full of life and love.

They were needed here to tend to the cherubs and were such a source of renewal and joy for the elders as well.

There were many times the higher angels would seek out Jillian and Wendy. The Angel of Peace was most fond of them. She often would spend time with them upon returning from an unusually difficult assignment. They had a magical way of soothing one's ruffled feathers. Other angels would also see such terrible sorrow. It would be Wendy and Jillian who could always be relied upon to rejuvenate everyone. No, the kingdom surely could not do without the two of them! This task was too much to ask of any one angel. After all, they were not human and already knew the secret to life. Why should they be subjected to such suffering?

"Oh, look over there on the seashore, Wendy, there's Joy. Let's go see her." Jillian had already started soaring towards the shore. "Saved by the bell," Jillian thought. It was difficult for Wendy to stay annoyed with Jillian at the sight of Joy. Joy was like a beloved mother to the two of them. When they were younger Wendy and Jillian were always under her wing. No matter where Joy's current assignments took her she often would bring the two of them along. In the beginning they could offer little assistance, yet as time passed they became more and more proficient and eventually were deemed ready for guardianship. They were then assigned to specific souls who were the most lacking in joy. From an angelic point of view they were quickly becoming experts on the subject and were relentless in their pursuit of joy for all. Although angels by nature are not prideful, Joy was aware she came dangerously close to expressing this feeling when it came to Wendy and Jillian, her beloved protégé's.

Angels need not express their thoughts in words. They can simply transmit a thought and the recipient will know what they are thinking as well as what they are feeling. Therefore, if an angel is caught off guard their feelings can become transparent. Such was the case with the Angel of Joy this day. The Angel of Joy was so consumed with protecting her own thoughts she did not think to camouflage her immediate feelings. Perhaps, this was the reason both Wendy and Jillian sensed all was not well with their beloved Joy. It was never appropriate for an angel to openly pry into another angel's feelings. This was especially true when one could sense the other was not ready to talk, out loud, about those things they would not share with their minds.

"Oh, Joy, it is so good to see you!" cried Wendy. "When did you get back? We have missed you so. We have heard so many rumors! The Elders say conditions are getting much worse on earth. While you were gone Jesus called for all of us to be thinking about ways in which to save more souls."

"Oh yes, Joy, and guess what? Wendy even put a suggestion in the golden box," Jillian chided. Wendy cringed as she had no intention of telling the Angel of Joy what she had done, especially after having recently been the brunt of Jillian's antics.

Wendy and Jillian were surprised Joy did not inquire as to the nature of Wendy's suggestion. In fact, Joy did her best to steer the conversation away from the topic altogether. Instead, she told them of the recent visit she had with one of her beloved humans, Sister Teresa.

There were, you see, certain humans assigned to senior angels. It was the Angel of Joy's privilege to watch over Sister Teresa. Wendy and Jillian had heard much about Sister Teresa over the years. Anjeze Gonxhe Bojaxhiu was her given name. "At the age of 12," Joy said, "Anjeze listened to her Father's call and knew her vocation would be to serve the poor." The Angel of Joy knew she would become the personification of joy on earth. For this reason Wendy and Jillian were always inquiring as to her welfare. At the age of eighteen Anjeze joined a community of Irish nuns in a mission in Calcutta.

It was there she took the name of Sister Teresa. For the past seventeen years she had been teaching at the Loreto Convent School in Calcutta and last they had heard was headmistress. That is why they were most alarmed when they heard she had fallen ill with tuberculosis. Joy had recently returned from visiting Sister Teresa. The Angel of Joy was sent to watch over her during this time. Many times Sister Teresa would feel a soothing warmth as Joy hovered at her bedside. Jesus had informed Joy of His plans for Anjeze since the beginning.

The Angel of Joy knew this was the time when Sister Teresa would answer His call. It was on her way to the town of Darjeeling, where she was being sent to recover, that Sister Teresa was to know what was to be the Father's desire for her.

Wendy and Jillian were filled with anticipation. "Oh my!" exclaimed Jillian. I am so excited! What is it she is to do?"

"Well, my dear ones, it was while she was on the train she heard our Father and was asked to give up all and follow Him to the slums!"

"Does that mean she will have to leave the order?" asked Wendy.

"Yes, Wendy it does." The Angel of Joy could tell they were most distressed to hear Sister Teresa would be leaving the order in Calcutta, as angels are especially fond of nuns because nuns, like angels, openly love the Father and live only to serve Him on earth. "I see you are distressed to hear she will be leaving the order. You must understand our Father has very special plans for her. She will accomplish much on earth and will teach many souls about joy; of this you can be certain. You must always remember my little ones there are many ways to serve our heavenly Father.

Those who are truly listening to His voice will know what they are called to do. In times like these, when there is so much pain and sorrow on earth, our Father depends on those who will understand what they are destined for. You will hear of many wonderful works to be done under Sister Teresa's tutelage over the years to come."

"If this was to be her calling why did she join the order?" asked Jillian, "Why didn't she just set about to serve the poor in the beginning?"

"You must understand my child, to be on earth and discover what a human is called to do, there is a period of learning, a period in which to understand what is one's gift and to acquire the knowledge and wisdom to use that gift. You might say then there are two parts to a human's journey. **The first half is spent in learning and the second half is spent practicing what they have learned.** This is a very simplistic way of putting it, yet in truth it is as simple as that. However, there are many souls who do not listen to the inner voice within. They disregard the promptings of their soul."

Wendy and Jillian loved to hear about the various humans for whom the Angel of Joy was guardian over. For, as her name implied, she was always assigned to those whom Jesus knew would exemplify joy. They had been hearing about Sister Teresa for a very long time. Jesus and the Angel of Joy both knew full well what she would accomplish on earth.

There were others whom Joy talked about as well. There was another human by the name of Dorothy Day who was giving her quite a challenge in the overall scheme of things. It seems Dorothy Day was very out-spoken! Lately she had been causing quite a stir among the Catholic Church. Her pacifist approach to World War II was not a popular stance. Although the Angel of Joy agreed with her position, it did create a myriad of com-plications. Dorothy had not always been of the Catholic faith. In her early years she was not the model saint others would come to know her as later in life. She was a prime example of what Jesus had always maintained.

He said human beings actually experienced two distinct journeys in life. Such was the case with Dorothy. Joy knew Dorothy's colorful past would be the exact catalyst to bring her close to Christ. Her illegitimate child is what caused her to have a conversion and cement her relationship with the Catholic Church. For Dorothy, religion was her solace. It was what brought her comfort in times of trial.

And so it was Wendy and Jillian were to grow to love and know such special humans through the stories the Angel of Joy would share with the two of them. When time permitted they would beg Joy for the latest updates upon her return from earth. They would barrage Joy with a million questions, as was the case on this day. However, the conversation on this particular day was abruptly drawn to a close as Joy was being summoned by St. Michael himself.

Over the years Wendy and Jillian had talked about what it would be like to live life as a human, much the same as a human would wonder what it would be like to be an angel. Although they had been the guardians of many a human over the years, they often wondered what it would be like to experience the emotions of a human being. Of the two it was Wendy who was the most curious. Perhaps this curiosity stemmed from the desire to understand why it was humans had such a difficult time with free will. Wendy thought free will or no free will they should desire to do what they were sent to do. It couldn't be that hard. All one had to do was pay attention to the promptings of their soul. It was so difficult for her to understand because as an angel she only longed to do what was pleasing to her heavenly Father. To do otherwise was simply unthinkable to Wendy.

Many times when riding the waves they would talk about such humans as Dorothy Day. "I tell you Jillian, I do not know why she didn't realize the man she was with was no good. No reasonable human would ever take up with an atheist! If I had been in charge of guarding her I would have interfered long before a child was conceived!"

"Yes, Wendy and that is precisely why St. Michael and our heavenly Father wouldn't assign such important people to us. If it hadn't been for this child and her lover's strong opposition to her faith, perhaps Dorothy would not have developed such a close relationship with our Father. I can imagine the trouble we would have been in with St. Michael. You know how he feels about our interfering."

"I personally am glad we haven't been given a guardian assignment for awhile," Wendy admitted. The last time we were on assignment I felt as if St. Michael were breathing down our necks. I told you we shouldn't have interfered with our charge, more precisely, Suzanne's wedding! St. Michael was very angry when he found out we let the air out of all four of the groom's tires hoping he wouldn't show up for the wedding. I must admit I never thought he would steal someone else's car to get there! I also didn't know that he would run over a pedestrian in the process!"

"Wendy, it's not funny!" lashed back Jillian. "The whole thing was your idea. We haven't been asked to go on another assignment since. I was so mortified when the other guardians heard about us being pulled from assignments indefinitely."

"Oh, Jillian, lighten up!" exclaimed Wendy. "St. Michael will get over it soon. You know he needs all of the experienced guardians he can get during these times. Why Joy herself is working hours on end. Not to worry, in the meantime, let's enjoy the break. You know there is no place like this on earth."

"Oh, I suppose you're right," Jillian responded, "but I still feel as though the others are laughing at us behind our backs. You know that no other angels have ever been banned from guardianship as long as we have."

Little did Wendy and Jillian realize they were in fact the reason St. Michael had summoned the Angel of Joy. After Jesus had spoken with Joy, regarding the two of them, St. Michael was summoned to Jesus. When he heard what Jesus was thinking he couldn't help but wonder if Jesus was suffering from overload. It was just that Michael couldn't believe His ears.

St. Michael was in charge of all the guardian angels. At times he too was called to earth to oversee certain situations; generally they would be major events. For example, during the great depression he was called to earth on numerous occasions. Far too many souls were committing suicide after losing their life's savings. These were the humans whose souls were in grave danger.

Jillian 2/2012

St. Michael was to protect as many souls as possible, for to take one's own life was considered the gravest of sins. How could a soul attain enlightenment when they did not complete what they were destined to do? These were trying times indeed, as there were so many souls who had lost sight of the true meaning of life. They had been distracted by the wiles of materialism. Wiser souls understood this was a time to draw even closer to our heavenly Father, confident He would provide for their needs.

St. Michael stood watch from above over special dignitaries, such as the President of the United States. He knew that people such as the President were responsible for millions of lives. However, there were other times St. Michael would be called to earth. These would be the times when specific guardian angels called upon him for assistance. Last but not least he could be called to earth unexpectedly when he suspected an angel was interfering with the will of a human. This, of course, was to be expected with a novice angel but not to be expected of such seasoned guardians as Wendy and Jillian.

Even though St. Michael had reason to be annoyed with the two of them, at times, he was quite fond of Wendy and Jillian. They were loved in the kingdom by all. Ironically, the same qualities the others loved them for were the very same qualities that caused them serious problems as guardians. Why, they simply wanted everyone and every being to be filled with joy. It was extremely difficult for them to stand by and watch humans make the wrong choices. In heaven one did not have the same type of choices to make because angels always chose to do what was in harmony with others.

When the Angel of Joy arrived she could see St. Michael was most agitated. St. Michael's eyes were the color of the deepest sapphire. When he was in battle his eyes could pierce even the most ferocious of enemies. It was safe to say there were many in the heavens who would not dare to do battle with him. These very same piercing eyes could be the gentlest eyes when he was moved, yet today his eyes portrayed a different message. Yes, one would say, a message of grave concern. So deep was his concentration that he did not even hear Joy when she arrived.

"Hello, St Michael," said Joy. "It has been awhile since we have seen each other. It seems one of us is always going in a different direction these days. Well, I wouldn't say a different direction necessarily. There are so many souls who need assistance now. I can only wonder at how the others are fairing with the increased work load. I have been wondering how St. Peter is?" Although she was curious as to why St. Michael had summoned her, she was most anxious to hear how their friend St. Peter was fairing. She knew what a difficult task he had.

Thank heavens she did not have to witness the arrival of so many souls. There were far too many souls who arrived at heaven's gates only to be disappointed with the results they achieved during their stay on earth. These were the same souls she said goodbye to prior to their journey on earth; the same souls who were so confident they would succeed this time. It was St. Peter's job to show them what they had accomplished on earth. Not that all of it was bad, it was just that in most cases many had lost sight of what was the reality and what was the truth, the very reason for their journey in the first place.

"As a matter of fact I saw him yesterday," answered St Michael. "I was escorting another soul to heaven's gate, one whose journey was cut short by the hideous acts of war. I tried to save him but in the end he chose to sacrifice his life to save another. I am sure his selfless acts of heroism will certainly be rewarded in heaven. I could see there were many who had arrived whose souls had not accomplished their purpose.

It is St. Peter who has to witness their disappointment as the events of their life flash before them. I tell you, my dear Joy, these killings are so senseless. When will mankind ever learn? There are so many who have been put in harm's way. Sometimes, I wish Jesus would just hurry and end things now. He is adamant mankind be given more chances. If I was Him I would have pulled the plug a long time ago. You would think man would have learned his lesson. You would think man would realize he is at the mercy of our Savior. Perhaps we have all seen too much. Perhaps we are all too weary. I am sorry you were asking me about St. Peter? He is a most amazing Saint indeed. You will get a chance to inquire of him yourself as Jesus has informed me He will be calling all of us together very soon.

I imagine you are wondering why I called you here? I know how busy you are. Jesus told me He mentioned, to you, the idea He has been thinking about. No offense, but if this is an example of His *Great Plan* we are in for quite a time?"

St. Michael had been telling Jesus for some time he was more than ready to join the others in battle against Satan. He was tired of Satan's senseless killings. He was tired of so many souls being deceived by his subtle tactics.

At times St. Michael felt Jesus was far too patient. These were desperate times and according to Jesus it was to get far worse before it would get better. Perhaps that is why Jesus was coming up with such a far out idea. Desperate times call for desperate measures.

"Did He tell you what He was thinking of? Is it not the most preposterous of ideas?" questioned St. Michael.

The Angel of Joy instinctively knew St Michael was talking about the Father's plan to create what would come to be known as an *earth angel*. She could also sense by his posture he felt the same way about this idea as she had. Joy experienced a wave of relief, as she realized St. Michael was in her corner. The very thought of having St. Michael as an adversary, on this issue, could be less than comforting.

"I can see you feel the same as I do, St. Michael," said Joy. "I do not know how our Father can consider such a thing. Nothing of this nature has ever been done before. I can see so many reasons why it would not succeed. First, the very thought of expecting an angel to reside in a humans body for any length of time is unheard of.

Second, an angel is designed to do our Father's will. How can anyone predict an *earth angel* will not succumb to free will? How then, I ask you, would it be possible for an angel to accomplish what the Father is asking when they have been given the same free will as a human? There are so many temptations on earth, as you and I know. It would only be a matter of time before Satan would get wind of what Jesus was doing and then the *earth angel* would surely fail. Even the most seasoned of angels would be hard pressed to succeed."

"I do quite agree." Michael answered. "We must be prepared with these arguments for I am certain this is under serious consideration. I feel this will be discussed at the meeting He is putting together. You and I must be of like minds on this subject. I do not know what St. Peter would think of this, yet I would like to feel he and the others would side with us!"

St. Michael had not mentioned Wendy or Jillian in the conversation. Perhaps, Jesus had merely shared the concept of *earth angels* with Michael without mentioning who He had in mind. Joy should have realized this was not the case as Wendy and Jillian were more schooled in the art of joy than the others. Surely, if St. Michael had heard who Jesus had in mind he would have more than enough arguments ready. If their past experience as guardians was any indication she was certain St. Michael would never agree on this basis alone. Michael knew what Joy was thinking.

"Yes, my friend," said St. Michael. "I know who He has in mind and I agree they are not suitable candidates, either one of them. They are far too independent and their love of life would cause them no end of problems in the world. If I cannot count on them as guardians, how could Jesus count on them for such an assignment, I ask?"

Although what St. Michael was saying was true, Joy realized these characteristics were exactly why Jesus was considering one or both of her mentees for this assignment. Although the Angel of Joy did not want them to go for maternal reasons, she did agree if any two could accomplish such a feat it would be the two of them. Her arguments were of a different nature.

She knew all too well the sorrows of humans. She knew firsthand the tactics Satan was using and what a formidable foe he would be. More than anything, she could not bear the thought of losing contact with Wendy or Jillian. Certainly, she could watch over them but as humans they could not converse with angels. She would have to stand by and watch as they made choices, as humans, they never would have even considered as angels. No, her reasons were entirely different.

Even though Michael didn't say as much, she knew how much he loved them. He, too, knew of their innocence and how fragile they both could be at times. Yes, Joy was certain he would do all he could to see they did not go.

Jesus knew of the meeting between the Angel of Joy and St. Michael. He knew the two of them thought Him to be crazy or at the very least desperate. Yet, after planting the seed He had much time to think about the details. He had time to formulate the answers to the questions He knew would be asked. Jesus knew of events to come that the others did not. He knew while there were those souls who knew the true meaning of joy and were doing great works, such as Sister Teresa and Dorothy Day, He also knew many souls could not relate to such selfless acts because so many souls had forgotten the reason for living. They had forgotten from where they came. So why could it not work? Why could He not send an angel to earth as one of them? Because the angels were created to serve Him, since the beginning, would they not remember what they were called to do? Jesus thought it was possible. So much would depend upon the characteristics of the angel.

Jesus had been working on the greatest plan of all time. He also realized Satan was using the knowledge humans had acquired as a means to deter souls from their calling. Jesus noticed humans were becoming more and more materialistic as a result. They were spending more and more time on the acquisition of things; things which would only distract them and separate them from their heavenly Father. It wasn't that Jesus did not want good things for His children. He wanted all of their needs to be fulfilled. In fact, if mankind shared their gifts with one another there would be more than enough for all of His children. Many hoarded what they had. They did not use what they had been given for the benefit of others.

Jesus hoped after the Great Depression Americans would be more appreciative of what they had and would share with those who were less fortunate, yet so many people still seemed to be bent on doing only what was for self. People were preoccupied with self after doing without during those difficult years. Oh, when would His children learn the essence of life? Why could they not grasp the art of living a joy filled life, a life which they had been created for? These were just some of the many thoughts which plagued Jesus daily.

Jesus knew of future events which would test the mightiest of souls. For this reason He was determined that all should be given every chance possible to come to Him. It seemed fewer and fewer of His children were coming to Him in prayer. Jesus loved to hear from His children as any parent does. Oh sure, there were the prayers that were sent in times of trouble but more and more, fewer and fewer were engaging in conversation with Him.

Unfortunately, He knew this communication would lessen even more in the coming years. There were many things He did not share with the angels. There were many sorrowful events that were yet to come. He did not want to burden them, yet somehow He must impress upon them the urgency of the times. He must get the others to understand now was the time to act. Now was the time to use new tactics. Now was the time to do what had never been done before. Jesus was determined good would prevail.

It is a most majestic sight when a group of angels are gathered together. When two angels are together it can be overwhelming as the light which resonates from their being is so bright. It is as though billions of fireflies are gathered together, their lights flickering in unison, a light so bright it can be seen throughout the universe. Even if the others in the kingdom had not heard rumors of the meeting Jesus had called, they would have known something special was happening, for it would be impossible not to notice the luminescent light transmitting throughout the heavens.

All of the elders in the kingdom had been called together, as well as the Senior Angels, including of course

St. Michael, St. Peter, the Angel of Joy and many others who served Jesus. There were too many to mention, yet all who served were in attendance this day. Even the Angel of Peace had been called home. This in itself was most unusual as there was much unrest on earth. Although the war was finally over, there were still those who sought to destroy life. There were still those gearing up for more. Yes, earth needed much guidance in the future. There was talk of a new bomb which, if allowed to be used, could destroy mankind forever. For this reason the Angel of Peace was most surprised to have been summoned away at this time. Then again most everyone who had been called from their assignments was surprised. There hadn't been a meeting of this magnitude since the great flood. Could it be that Jesus was planning a similar event?

Wendy and Jillian had heard Jesus was planning a very important meeting. They knew things had not been going well of late. They'd heard rumors of Jesus' Great Plan, yet they had no idea He was about to implement the beginning stages of such a plan. Had either of them known they were to be part of this plan perhaps they would have been tempted to listen in, or should we say eavesdrop? And so it was they spent most of the day playing with the cherubs in the meadow. They so loved spending time with the littlest of angels, for it was when they were with the cherubs each was most content. One could hear the gentle tinkling of bells from afar. An angel's laughter was such a melodious sound and could be heard across heaven.

Jillian 7/2012

The Angel of Joy could hear the laughter, as could the others. It was this laughter that was the opening for the next subject on the agenda. The meeting had been called to order by St. Michael. Each Senior Angel had just finished giving their update of the overall progress being made by mankind in specific categories. Although there were those who were getting it, the general consensus was there were far too many who were in jeopardy. Why, just the report from the Angel of Peace was enough to ruffle the feathers of even the most seasoned angel. When she spoke of the bomb mankind had created, Joy, could see St. Michael's eyes flash with anger.

She could tell St. Michael was more than ready to do battle. After this report no one could blame Jesus if He did a repeat of the great flood. Mankind did not deserve Jesus' unending mercy.

There were many other disturbing reports as well. The Angel of Compassion told of the works of Sister Teresa. Although her works were well known by the angels, there were far too many who would not follow her example. There was such poverty on earth. There were far too many who were not willing to share with the less fortunate. Why was it humans did not understand **every time they connected with another human being they were responsible for sharing their gifts and talents with one another?** The angels knew there were more than enough gifts to go around. Each human had been blessed with their very own special gifts by the Father.

This meeting was not one only of gloom. On the contrary, there were many good works reported, yet Jesus and the others knew there were those in the world who would seek to destroy. They, too, knew there would come a time when the final battle would be fought.

It is important at this point to understand time in the angelic realm, our Father's kingdom, is not the same as time is to a human on earth. A lifetime for a human is but a fleeting moment in our Father's kingdom. Therefore, what would seem like an eternity in one's human life is but a short span of time in the kingdom. To Jesus and the others now was the time to take action. Now was the time to put into place those actions that were necessary to insure as many souls as possible were saved.

When Jesus spoke all in attendance came to full attention. *"My dear ones, thank you for coming today. I know how busy all of you are and how very difficult it* *is to pull away from your work. I have listened to your reports and I thank you for your updates. While there is a great deal to be concerned about, I am confident we can work together and accomplish much in the years to come, but we must be willing to do that which has not been done before. We must be willing to take steps which will allow more souls to accomplish that which they have been called to do. For when this is done **My kingdom shall reign on earth**! It is time now to put on our armor. I know St. Michael is more than ready to lead My legion in the heavens against Lucifer. While I, too, am anxious for his fall to take place, we must do all we can to save My precious souls. Time is running out and soon there will be no more chances. So, while I know it is tedious and I know some are becoming impatient, I have an idea I believe will work. I have discussed this idea with St. Michael and with the Angel of Joy. What I would like to do is send a legion of angels to earth in human form. These earth angels will be skilled in various subjects. These subjects will focus on a variety of attributes, the same attributes many of you specialize in. For example, some angels are experts on the subject of joy. These angels will live life as humans and will be given the gift of free will as any human would be given. Since they have known nothing but My will prior to this point, I believe they will succeed in their task. They must be free to experience life the same as any human. They must be free to grow and to acquire the knowledge they need in order to accomplish what they have been sent to do."* Jesus could tell by the look on the other's faces they were perplexed. He also knew they had many concerns and was prepared to answer whatever questions were thrown at Him.

The first to speak out was His beloved friend St. Michael. Since He had discussed this idea with Michael, He knew St. Michael would have much to say. He, however, was not prepared for St. Michael's abrupt response.

"It cannot work! How can you expect an angel to do strictly Your will on earth and allow them free will? Everyone knows once Satan finds out about this he will use every tactic to destroy them. This in itself would be unfair. No matter how much love they have for You, my friend, what You are asking is not reasonable. You will be asking them to live as normal human beings. It would be one thing if they were sent on a specific assignment, such as Sister Teresa or even Dorothy Day. What you are asking is that they be sent to earth to teach others about joy in a secular setting. Why could they not teach about joy under the sanctity of the church? There is much work to be done in this regard. At least they would not be thrown out amongst the wolves."

"I understand your concerns, Michael," responded Jesus, *"but these angels must be free to choose the road they wish to take on earth. They must be able to reach those who do not attend church, for there are many who attend who do not know the true meaning of joy either. I know that I can count on you to watch over them. I will send others to them throughout their lives to offer assistance whenever necessary. When they are ready I am prepared to go to them as well.*

Truly, there are miraculous people on earth who do great works. Yet, there are millions of souls who do not desire to follow such a path, and even if they have the desire they do not feel capable of such acts. No, these earth angels must be ordinary and believable! They must be allowed to live life as any human being is allowed."

The Angel of Joy knew full well Jesus had made up His mind on the subject. She could tell He had given this matter a great deal of thought and was prepared to respond to any questions they might have. She also knew once He had made up His mind there was no dissuading Him, and so it was she decided to support His decision. She could only hope that she could persuade Him to postpone His decision until she was certain the prospective *earth angels* had been fully versed on the subject of joy. She was certain He was considering her beloved Wendy and Jillian for the task. If this was to happen she wanted them to have every advantage which would require in-depth training of a different kind, more so than in the past. They would need to know much more about life as humans. Even though they both had been guardians of humans in the past, they had never experienced free will. They would be exposed to temptations they could never have considered as angels.

"While I can't say it will work, Father," responded Joy, "I can't say for certain it can't be done. My biggest concern is that they will be asked to live in two worlds, Jesus. Will they not feel as though they never belong? Will they not feel as though they have one foot in each world?"

"Perhaps, My Joy," Jesus answered, *"but because they have worked for Me and only Me in the past, I believe they will listen to what they have been called to do. I will make certain they are given the opportunity to do so."* Jesus could tell the others were becoming impatient.

"I thank you all for coming. I appreciate your reports. It is because of these reports I am convinced it is time to take the beginning steps in My plan to bring My kingdom to earth. I am asking each of you to think of those candidates whom you feel would be able to succeed at such an endeavor."

The meeting was now adjourned. Many in the kingdom were gravely concerned. If this first idea was any inkling of what the Father's plan consisted of they were in for quite a time of it. Never had they heard of such a notion, not in all of eternity. It was too much to ask of any one angel. After all, why should any angel be asked to take on such a task?

No one was anxious to nominate anyone. Jesus knew His angels well and as a result He was certain no names would be given, not because they were not supportive of Him, but because there was much they did not know about the future. As much as they were guardians of humans, he was guardian of His angels; therefore, He did not want them to worry about what was to come. If times were different Jesus would not make such a request of His beloved angels. He knew something had to be done to teach His earthly children the purpose for their being.

Souls were crying out daily now. They were so anxious to return to the Father. Many souls were becoming very discouraged as they had lost sight of what their mission was on earth. Yet, whoever was to be an *earth angel* needed to know from the deepest center of their being what they were sent to do. This was something that had never been done before. This would be a very important assignment. He knew if any two angels could succeed it would be Wendy and Jillian.

Jesus was not surprised to see Joy waiting for Him in the garden. He knew how difficult this task would be for her. He knew of the love she had for the two of them and that they would be sorely missed. He was willing to let her take all the time she needed in order to prepare them for the journey which lie ahead. He knew she would insure they were well schooled in every aspect of joy. So much would need to be done to get them ready for the transition.

"Joy, how fitting it is to find you here," said Jesus. *"This is My favorite place in all of My kingdom. This is the very place the idea of an earth angel came to mind. I do so love the fragrance of jasmine as it reminds Me of My angels; My special flock who are so loyal to Me; loyal even when I know what I ask is causing them great pain, as it is with you My little one."* Jesus reached for the Angel of Joy's hand as He could see the tears brimming in her eyes. He knew instantly they were not the tears of joy for which she was so well known. They were tears brought about by immense concern, the kind of concern only a mother's love can bring.

St. Michael was most anxious to leave the meeting. There was so much for him to think about. He, too, knew it was just a matter of time before Wendy and Jillian were to hear about the Father's plan. He also knew in his heart they were the best candidates for the job or He would never ask the two of them to leave heaven for an earthly life. They were a bothersome duo, that was for sure, yet Michael had such a soft spot in his heart for the two of them and their childlike antics. The kingdom would surely miss them. The only consolation for St. Michael, in the scheme of things, was that he would insure that he personally would be able to oversee their stay on earth. No mortal harm would come to the two of them if he had anything to say about it. He would not let Satan harm them; that for was certain. He knew how upset the Angel of Joy was. Although, she openly supported Jesus in the meeting, he knew what it was costing her inside.

And so Michael went looking for Joy. He wanted to console her. He, the guardian angel of all angels, would personally watch over Wendy and Jillian. He would let Jesus know his intentions as well. He saw the two of them talking in the garden. It looked as if the Angel of Joy had been crying. Yes, thought St. Michael, this was going to be very hard on his dear friend. Michael did not want to interrupt the two of them and was debating whether he should leave unannounced; of course He should have known Jesus would sense his presence.

"Michael, I thought you were here. Don't be bashful (as if he ever was). I knew you would come. I was just thanking Joy for her support. I know how hard this is

on the two of you. I have assured Joy she can take all the time she needs to make Wendy and Jillian ready for this assignment," explained Jesus.

It was decided the Angel of Joy would be the one to approach Wendy and Jillian with the idea. They would not be forced to do anything they did not want to do. Jesus knew this would not be an easy decision for these two angels. There were many questions which could not be answered, yet He knew of their loyalty to Him. He also knew of their intense love for one another.

Wendy and Jillian were to arrive on earth at separate times. One would lead the way and the other would follow. That way whatever wasn't learned by one would be learned by the other. It would be necessary for them to be brought into two totally different families; what one family did not provide the other would.

When a soul is sent to earth it is matched up with a specific family, a family that will provide each soul the opportunity to accomplish their mission. In a human's eyes it can seem as if some souls were sent into the most bizarre and unlikely surroundings, yet these surroundings, these families if you will, are the catalyst for the growth they will need to accomplish their purpose. Because Wendy and Jillian would teach others the art of joy, each would need to bring the knowledge they had acquired to the task. Each one would need to be on earth a distinct period of time before they met, to acquire a body of knowledge which would insure together they would succeed.

Wendy had always wondered what it would be like to be a human. Many times she had watched her beloved humans as they journeyed through life. She wondered what it would be like to fall madly and completely in love with another being. What would it would be like to experience childbirth and have a child of her own? She had witnessed so much over the ages; humans with their short comings; humans who became satiated with the many enticements the world offered. What would it be like to experience the five senses, to actually experience the touch of a human? Yes, there was so much she had wondered about over the years. Never in her wildest dreams had she really desired to be a human. Wendy had never truly desired to become one with the flesh. No, she and Jillian had seen the temptations which plagued humans. They saw how the souls of most humans were neglected. All considered, they were very content to work for the Father.

They knew first hand there was no place on earth to compare to His heavenly kingdom. While one can reflect on the most beautiful place on earth and magnify it a trillion times over, it still could never compare to what awaits one in paradise. Every color imaginable is represented in the heavens. All one need do is look at the brilliance of a rainbow to get a slight glimpse of what awaits them. Field after field of flowers garnish the luscious green meadows. Ruby red tulips scatter themselves among pockets of vibrant lilies ranging in colors from yellow to brilliant orange. Colorful daisies dance among the tulips swaying side by side with bright yellow daffodils.

Jillian 7/2012

Every flower one has ever seen is represented in the Father's kingdom. The smell of jasmine laced with honeysuckle abounds in the air, tantalizing the senses.

The sea breeze blows ever so gently throughout the kingdom while seagulls soar over head, trilling their welcome to all. The sea surrounds the heavens on all sides. Warm waves embrace the seashore, gently lapping to and fro atop the golden sand. White sand sparkles in the sunlight as though a million diamonds had been scattered about.

There is no sense of urgency in our Father's kingdom, as all is well. Love permeates the air and every being. Heaven is perfection in its purest sense. Heaven is home to the angels, for this is their kingdom. There is no sorrow, only joy. Evil does not exist. There is only good and as a result, angels have no desire to be anywhere else. They can, however, understand why a human would have difficulty fathoming what the Father has in store for them. Human beings have no recollection from where they have come from. If they did they could not bear to remain on earth.

Jesus, St. Michael and The Angel of Joy were so caught up in the recent decision it never occurred to them that Wendy or Jillian might not want to go. They both had such an adventuresome spirit. Jesus knew they would both be anxious to be part of such an important experiment, for an experiment it truly was. No one, not even Jesus, knew for certain His idea would actually work.

When Jesus and the Angel of Joy approached Wendy and Jillian they could not help but smile. Wendy had covered her eyes with the tips of her wings while Jillian turned her round and round. Any passerby would be amused to see how deeply engrossed in a game of blind man's bluff these grown angels were. The cherubs who were filled with anticipation tinkled with glee as they scampered about the meadow seeking a place in which to hide. Wendy and Jillian loved the little cherubs as if they were their own. They were so innocent and so full of life. For Wendy and Jillian, the cherubs were the very essence of joy. So engrossed were they in their pursuit of the little ones they did not see Jesus and the Angel of Joy standing under the voluminous oak tree. Only when the littlest cherub had been found did Jillian notice the two of them standing there.

Jillian 2012

"Oh my goodness, Wendy," exclaimed Jillian, "look who's here! It's Jesus and Joy! Wendy quickly lowered the tips of her wings.

"Oh, what a surprise," Wendy chimed. Jesus was so busy these days it was indeed a special occasion for Him to visit. In fact, the last time Wendy had seen Him was prior to her submitting her rather startling suggestion.

"Oh my," she thought. "Why is He here? Oh and why is the Angel of Joy with Him?" Wendy was most concerned Jesus was put out about her suggestion regarding free will. If His reaction was even half of what Jillian's was He must think her quite the fool. Perhaps, that is why He asked the Angel of Joy to accompany Him on this visit. Wendy was certain she was in for quite a talking to. She was so certain of what was to come that she was totally taken back when she heard the true reason for His visit.

"Well, hello there My precious ones," said Jesus, *"I see you are busy entertaining the cherubs! I am hard pressed to see who is having more fun, the cherubs or yourselves."* Jesus so loved the little cherubs. He knew how much Wendy and Jillian meant to the little ones of His kingdom, for in so many ways they were like children themselves. Perhaps, that is why St. Michael and the others were so protective of the two of them. One never knew for certain what the two of them were up to. Personally, He was glad when St. Michael pulled them from their guardianship duties. He loved seeing them here like this with the cherubs. They brought joy to so many in the kingdom. The very reason He had chosen them for this assignment was the very reason they were so loved by the others. Perhaps, this was why He had such a difficult time making His decision, for Jesus had spent countless hours mulling over the details of this most unique assignment. He did not want to subject them to a task that could overly tax their beautiful spirits, yet while He knew this

would be no easy assignment, in truth, there were no others in the kingdom more suitable than Wendy and Jillian.

Jillian could sense Wendy's discomfort as her friend was rendered speechless. "Oh Jesus, Wendy and I are so glad you are here. This is such a treat for us. We know how busy you have been. Are you hungry? Is there something we can get you to eat? Oh Joy, what a delight to see you as well. It seems as though it has been such a long time since you have come to visit."

Jillian knew she was rambling, for in truth, she was most anxious as to the reason for their visit. Even though she had laughed at Wendy's suggestion, she couldn't imagine that was why Jesus and Joy had sought them out. Usually, when Joy wanted to see them she would let them know in advance of her coming. This time such was not the case.

"No, thank you Jillian, we ate before we came," Joy replied. Joy could see they were most uncomfortable. She wanted to put the two of them at ease as she knew they were worried about the suggestion Wendy had submitted. "There is something Jesus and I wanted to talk to the two of you about."

"Perhaps, you heard of My recent meeting held with the other Senior Angels?" Jesus asked. *"As you may have heard more and more souls on earth are becoming increasingly discouraged. It is becoming more difficult for souls to achieve their mission in life because as man's knowledge increases so do the earthly distractions. These distractions fill mankind's time with*

Godless activities. Humans no longer take time to hear that which comes from the center of their being and as a result religion is becoming less and less popular. I, foresee a time in the near future when churches will be frequented by few and as a result many children will not know Me. I have been thinking of a plan for some time now. There is much to come which I am afraid will tempt many souls. I need My children on earth to understand the true meaning of joy. I need them to remember from whence they came. While some on earth exemplify joy, many cannot relate to their joyful spirits. If times are difficult now I am afraid, they will get worse instead of better. All of My guardians are working over-time, as you know."

Wendy and Jillian now felt they understood why Jesus and the Angel of Joy had come. Wendy had said it was just a matter of time before St. Michael acknowledged the error of his decision, and they would be reinstated to guardianship status. They sent a knowing glance to one another quite certain of what was to come. Jesus had just said the guardians were working overtime and they too were most discouraged.

Perhaps, St. Michael now realized they were just the type of guardians the world needed; guardians who would see to it their humans accomplished their earthly missions. After all, these were desperate times. Surely, guardians with their experience were in high demand. Thinking back on it now, Wendy and Jillian should have known that was not the reason for Jesus' visit, for if this would have been the case St. Michael would have come himself. Also, a visit from Jesus was highly unusual these days as there was so much to be done.

*"What I am about to tell you I have shared with the Angel of Joy as well as the elders. I must tell you what I am about to propose has never been done before but I feel certain My plan can work. You both have been mentored by Joy for a considerable time now. If there are any in the kingdom who truly understand the art of joy-filled living I believe it is you. As guardians you have often taken much into your own hands. I am well aware of the difficulties in dealing with the choices humans make; choices which often seem unreasonable to angels such as you. It is difficult for an angel to fully under-stand the gift of free will. Yet, without this free will My children would not come to fully understand the true meaning of life. **Free will allows them to formulate their own lesson plans through the choices they make.** A life's journey is merely the highway to heaven. There are many routes one can choose. Depending on the route one takes, this ride can be relatively smooth or it can be bumpy at best. You, as My angels, desire only to serve Me and do that which is of My will, because you have been created for this specific purpose. You are enlightened beings and have always been so. I know many angels have wondered what it would truly be like to be human. Yet, I know of no angel who has truly desired to become human."*

Wendy wondered if somehow Jesus had been able to read her thoughts. She recalled the many times she had wondered what it would be like to be human. In fact, there were a few times she remembered secretly longing for this opportunity, for she was quite sure if she had been sent to earth as a human she would not fail, but would accomplish her life's purpose. No, she would not be one of those souls who had to return time after time. She would show the world the true meaning of joy. That was for certain!

Jillian, on the other hand, was more sympathetic to a soul's plight. She recently recalled telling Wendy how difficult she felt it would be for a human to believe in heaven. "Humans," she said, "were being asked to believe in what they could not see. At least a guardian angel knows of both worlds." Many times Jillian would express how unfair she felt this was to mankind.

Jesus was giving Wendy and Jillian time to digest what He was saying. In truth, there was nothing about His beloved angels He did not know. He knew their every thought. Jesus knew of Wendy's secret longing to experience life in the flesh. He also knew this was partly due to the frustration she felt when a soul did not accomplish their mission. It was one thing to wonder about something and quite another to actually be given the opportunity to fulfill ones secret longings.

Jillian, on the other hand, He knew loved her humans with all of her heart. She had never expressed a desire to experience life as a human. However, He felt she would rise quite well to the task should she be given an opportunity to do so.

Jesus had promised the Angel of Joy He would merely present the idea of *earth angels* to the two of them. He would not force either of them to go. He simply would lay out the details of His plan and wait to hear their response. The Angel of Joy was growing impatient. She knew Wendy and Jillian were about to burst with anticipation, yet they were, as angels often are, too polite to pry. Joy had stood silently by for as long as she could.

"What Jesus is saying is He thinks if an angel were to go to earth to teach about joy, she could have a great impact on mankind. She would be the catalyst which would set in motion the beginning of His kingdom on earth."

"But how could an angel do so? We are not to interfere with the choices our humans make. How can we get them to exemplify joy if they do not listen to what comes from the center of their being? You know how St. Michael feels about a guardian interfering in a human's life," Jillian questioned. "Jesus, haven't you always said humans must be free to choose their own lesson plan?"

"Yes, Jillian, this is true but I wasn't talking about guardians working through their humans. I was thinking about sending an angel to earth as a human. This angel would be schooled in the art of joy and would know she works for Me. She would be given the gift of free will, just as any human is given, so she would be able to experience life as any mortal does."

"But if she is given the gift of free will and does not have any special powers, how will she know what she is to do?" questioned Wendy. "What would make this angel any different than any other human? Old soul or not, there are many who fail even when they do realize what their purpose is. Would this angel do works like that of Sister Teresa?"

Jesus could tell by the myriad of questions Wendy was spouting He had indeed peeked her interest. He also knew there were many questions that would need answering. This was not an endeavor to be taken lightly.

"Your questions are indeed valid My little ones. It would take the right angel to undertake such a task. There are certain qualifications I am looking for. One must exemplify joy that is for certain. Yet, this angel must understand the magnitude of the task at hand. She must demonstrate to Me her understanding of what the task would entail. This is not a decision to be made lightly, for once the process begins there will be no turning back. Much learning beforehand will be required to prepare for such an assignment. This angel must not have any doubts because there will be times in which I will seem very far away indeed. There will be times the Angel of Joy is far away as well, yet I will tell you whoever goes will be personally guarded by St. Michael himself. Also, the Angel of Joy will be avail-able whenever the need is felt. I, too, will always be there. I will do everything I can to insure this mission is successful. If this works with a few there will be more and more earth angels sent over time as a new form of guardian angels. Time is short and I want all souls to be made ready for My return. Whoever goes must under-stand she or they will be under great attack. Although I will do My best to insure Satan does not get wind of

this plan, it will only be a matter of time before he discovers what is going on."

Wendy did not dare look at Jillian. She knew her heavenly sister would be able to tell right away what she was thinking. Wendy knew she would love to do this for Jesus and for the many souls who were crying out for help, yet she knew this was a task she would not want to take on without Jillian.

Jillian was staring off into the distance lost in her own thoughts. She knew Wendy well enough to predict she would eagerly volunteer for such an assignment; Jillian on the other hand was not so eager. No, there were many questions to which she would need answers to first, although she had to admit it did sound somewhat exciting.

Ever since Wendy was a small cherub when she became excited she would wrap her wings around her body to keep them from fluttering up and down. This was a most difficult task as a full grown angel's wings are quite large, measuring well over 12 feet in width. By the times her wings encircled her body one could barely see the tip of her head. This was the posture she took now. Jillian knew this posture well and realized Wendy had already made up her mind. Jesus couldn't help smiling as He saw the two of them standing there. He could barely see the tip of Wendy's head. He could however see Jillian quite well and knew her enthusiasm did not match Wendy's. Of the two, it was Wendy who tended to wear her heart on her angelic shoulder; shoulders, He must admit, which were hard to see at the moment as they too were engulfed by her wings.

The Angel of Joy sensed Wendy's enthusiasm. She wondered how much Jesus had to do with such a response. She knew **enthusiasm, generally speaking, was merely a reflection of what the Father was calling each spirit to do**. Many times she had wondered at the folly of humans. If only they understood **what they are enthusiastic about, as well as what is the deepest desire of their heart; comes from their heavenly Father**. Now, as Joy thought back over time, Wendy had always shown a strong curiosity about life as a human. Many times, in fact, she had commented, "Oh, if only I were human I would know what I was called to do. I would succeed. I don't understand why a soul returns time and time again for the same lesson plan."

Even if Wendy had not engulfed herself in her wings as an open expression of the excitement she felt inside, the Angel of Joy was easily able to read Wendy's thoughts; in her enthusiasm Wendy's thoughts were transparent to all.

At this point Wendy could no longer contain herself and so it was without thinking she blurted out, "Oh Father, why not me? I would love to be able to go to earth to teach humans about joy! Many times I have been frustrated watching my assignees struggle so. I know with your help I could make a difference and, why, if Jillian were to come too, there would be no stopping us!" It was at this point Wendy noticed the alarm in Jillian's eyes.

Jillian 8/2012

She tried to tap into her thinking but Jillian had already
blocked Wendy and the others out, for in truth she was
quite skeptical. As a guardian of humans, Jillian had
seen how mankind struggled as a result of free will. Even
though she had never experienced life as a human, she

was certain it was not easy to accomplish one's spiritual assignment on earth. No, she would much rather stay right where she was. It wasn't that she didn't want to help the legion of souls who were struggling in these times; it was just that Jillian felt she could be of more use working directly in the Father's kingdom. After all, she and Wendy didn't really even make the best guardians of humans, if one wanted to be truthful.

Jesus knew Jillian would initially not be as enthused about this assignment as Wendy was, yet He was certain in time she too would come around. Actually, this would be for the best, as they could each learn their own lessons so when the time was right they could combine their knowledge and together accomplish their mission. It was for this reason Jesus intervened before Jillian had a chance to react to Wendy's enthusiastic response, for in truth He knew Jillian would not decline what He asked of His angels.

"Wendy, I am not surprised you show such an interest. I think you would be a wonderful candidate for this assignment. I am certain the two of you would do a terrific job. Yet, for the time being I think it would be better if only one of you were to go initially. It will take some time before you have the knowledge you need to accomplish your assignment, for as a human, you will be able to make many life choices which will affect what you learn. If all goes well, another angel could come at a later date to assist you with your duties." Even though Jesus was certain Jillian would be more than anxious to join Wendy later on, He did not want her to feel as if she did not have a choice.

Jillian on the other hand was having second thoughts about her initial response. She didn't like the thought of Wendy going first, after all she was just as capable as Wendy, if not more suitable in some ways. Also, she and Wendy had never been apart. Even when they were on different assignments they were only a thought away from each other. Angels can communicate with one another no matter what the distance. Many times even when they are in close proximity they do not waste time with verbal conversation, as it is much quicker to communicate via their thoughts.

Jillian knew once Wendy became human she would lose contact with her sister. Even though there were times she wondered what it would be like to be separated, Jillian never really even considered the possibility of this event. Now, not only did it seem to be possible it appeared as though it was quite likely to occur.

Jesus could see the distress in their eyes. He knew even though Wendy was very excited at the prospect of going, He also knew of their fondness for one another. Jesus knew all too well what it would mean for the two of them to be separated. He wanted to make certain Jillian truly desired this assignment. Yes, the time apart would do them good.

Personally, Joy was glad to hear Jesus did not plan on sending the two of them together at once; somehow the plan felt less risky this way. Also, the cherubs would still have Jillian to depend on. Wendy would be sorely missed from the kingdom, that was for certain, but to have the two of them gone at the same time would be a huge loss to the little ones as well as some of the elders. Yes, this would be the best way.

"I am going to leave you now. I want the two of you to have time to talk about this. There will be much training to be done beforehand. If you should have a change of heart, Wendy, you need only let Me know. Whoever takes this assignment must not have any doubts for once the wheels are put in motion there can be no turning back."

Joy wrapped her wings around her two dearest angels. She felt their trembling and knew what was transpiring in each of their hearts. "I am here for the both of you if you want to talk, but right now I think it is best if I leave the two of you to mull this over. I know Jesus wants you to have time to truly consider your decision, Wendy. I will be away for awhile as I have some urgent matters to attend to on earth. When I return, we will talk again."

The Angel of Joy knew this would be a most difficult decision for the two heavenly sisters. Even though she knew Wendy was most anxious to accept this assignment she also realized Jesus wanted her to have ample time to truly ponder what could be in store for her, as well as what her decision would mean to Jillian. The Angel of Joy was well aware of the perilous times on earth. She also understood mankind's reaction to those events. Many humans were acting out as a direct response to the harsh times they had experienced. As the Angel of Joy, Joy knew the essence of sorrow. Now, instead of sharing with those less fortunate, many were focused on amassing fortunes for themselves.

Joy was en route to earth now as one of her assigned humans had been sending urgent requests to the heavenly Father. Dorothy Day was one of Joy's favorites. She was tireless in her efforts to serve the poor, yet many times Dorothy had to understand not all were as zealous as she and as a result needed to be reminded more could be accomplished through selfless deeds than fiery words. This was difficult for Dorothy, as God had equipped her with the gift of writing, but at times she was far too outspoken for her own good.

Joy loved Dorothy's convictions, yet there were those in the church who were opposed to her insistence on pacifism even after the bombing of Pearl Harbor. It was the Angel of Joy's job to see to it Dorothy accomplished her mission on earth. Someday, Joy knew, if Dorothy stayed the course, she would be considered a saint by many. Joy also knew humans like Dorothy were far too few in number. Mankind was tired of doing without and was now interested in the material. She knew this condition could only get worse overtime as man focused on what he thought would bring him happiness. Joy was seeing more than ever before how humans were confusing happiness with joy.

Mankind was in the process of acquiring much technical knowledge. Joy had already seen how this knowledge would provide much distraction for humans. It would entertain them while keeping them from spending time with their Father. Joy was not able to see future events as the Father did. She too knew there were perilous times ahead. Man had not responded to past major events as

Jesus had hoped. Mankind was becoming more and more complacent. At this rate it would be a long time before His kingdom would reign on earth. There were greedy times ahead; she was certain of that.

Wendy and Jillian were glad to have this time alone. Each was lost momentarily in her own thoughts. Although they had many questions to ask of Jesus, they wanted to talk to one another. They knew Joy was on her way to earth. They also knew she guided some of the most precious humans on earth. What would be asked of them would be different from those who had gone before.

Instinctively the two of them headed for the seashore. When they were not floating atop the waves they loved to stroll along the water's edge. Often they would run into the water only to run back as the waves rippled over their feet. Angels are very childlike in nature and cannot resist taking part in nature's vast array of entertainment. Heaven is very entertaining. It offers the most sublime conditions in which to wile away the hours. It is not only the littlest of cherubs who take advantage of heaven's amenities. Often, one will see such angels as St. Michael or St. Peter running to and fro among the waves as well. Jesus knew even His most senior angels needed a source of respite. It was just a matter of angelic choice as to what the respite would be.

It was no surprise to Wendy and Jillian to see St. Peter frantically flapping his wings while attempting to remain atop the mounting onslaught of waves. Far ahead of him was St. Michael, who had already artfully descended upon the waters. It was a most humorous sight as St. Peter was

no match for Michael, the guardian of all heaven, who was built like the mightiest warrior.

St. Peter, on the contrary, had a lot of time on his hands, shall we say. As head keeper of heaven's gates, St. Peter's physical activities were somewhat limited. Everyone in the kingdom knew St. Peter's favorite pastime involved culinary activities. As a result, his bulky frame created quite a sight as he attempted to stay atop the waves. One might say he was having quite a time staying afloat. By the time Wendy and Jillian had arrived, St. Peter's wings were drenched with water. Normally, an angel's wings acted as floating devices, however, in the case of St. Peter, they had become anchors causing his body to sink below the waves. One could hear St. Michael laughing in the background as he observed his friend's most perilous flight. St. Peter saw no humor in the situation. He had already swallowed what seemed to be a gallon of salt water and was frantically anticipating what the next wave would bring. Hearing his friend's laughter did nothing to console him. If the truth be known, St. Peter was becoming concerned that he soon would be joining the urchins at the bottom of the sea.

It was at this point St. Michael noticed his friend's plight. Within a fraction of a second He had swooped St. Peter up out of the water, artfully placing him upright on the golden sand.

"Well, well," boomed St. Michael, "It appears as though you were on the brink of sinking! Perhaps I need to give you some swimming lessons my friend, or should I say floating lessons? Ha, ha! Can't say as I have ever seen the likes of an angel doing this before! What normally keeps one afloat in your case was soon to be your demise. Your wings are thoroughly drenched. It will take forever and a day to dry them out."

Normally, St. Peter would not be so acquiescent, as he was not known to accept St. Michael's barbs quietly, yet he was so grateful St. Michael came to his rescue that he simply nodded his head in agreement. It would have been better for St. Michael had he stopped while he was ahead. Michael, on the other hand, thought this an opportune time to bring up St. Peter's overall physical condition, drawing particular attention to his bulky waist line.

"You know, Peter, this would be an excellent time for you to consider eating a little less and spending a little more time exercising," Michael chided. "Just because you are an angel doesn't mean you should not care about your appearance. After all, you are the first angel one sees upon entering our Father's kingdom! If you were a human you would, I fear, suffer the physical chastisements of your affinity for food!"

Wendy and Jillian could see St. Peter was becoming most agitated and that this would be a perfect time to approach the two senior angels. They would have made themselves known sooner; however, it took them some time to compose themselves. Never had they witnessed such a humorous sight as St. Michael converging upon St. Peter. Even St. Peter's bulky frame looked like that of the littlest cherub next to St. Michael. Jillian was most concerned St. Peter could hear them laughing as they were unable to restrain themselves. It was Jillian who finally put the tip of her wing over Wendy's mouth as Wendy was tinkling with laughter from the tips of her toes to the top of her halo.

"Hi, you two, it looks like you just went for a swim!" Wendy chimed.

"Yes, we just got here," Jillian added. They never would embarrass St. Peter. If St. Peter even suspected they had witnessed such an event he would have been mortified. No, it was far better if they kept their knowledge to themselves. By now St. Peter had composed himself and was feeling more sociable.

"My, my, it is so good to see the two of you!" exclaimed St. Peter. "It has been quite awhile. You must be behaving yourselves as I haven't heard St. Michael go on about the two of you lately."

St. Peter knew, of course, this was because they had not been given a guardianship assignment for quite some time. He did not want them to know he was aware St. Michael had pulled them from their last assignment.

He, as well as Michael, had attended the recent meeting. St. Peter and Michael had discussed Jesus' plan at great length with Him and soon realized Jesus was not to be deterred from His idea. St. Peter felt it could work as he had seen many humans who had accomplished great feats on earth. True, they were few in number, but if *earth angels* could be guided, why wouldn't it work? *Earth angels* would have the advantage of intrinsically knowing they worked for Jesus. Over time, with the help of Joy and the Father, they could be guided to do what they had been created for. It was already decided the Angel of Joy would be the *earth angel's* guardian.

Neither, St. Peter nor Michael knew whether Jesus had approached Wendy or Jillian regarding His plans. St. Peter was never one to beat around the bush and so it was no surprise when he asked if either Wendy or Jillian had spoken to Jesus recently.

Wendy was not certain how to respond as she was not ready to share her decision with anyone yet. In her heart she knew what she wanted to do, yet she would not do or say anything until she knew how Jillian felt. Although she was longing to get their opinions, she was not all that anxious to hear what St. Michael would say. After all, he was the one who pulled them from their last assignment. She was certain he would think they were not capable.

Nothing could be farther from the truth. St. Michael, now seeing the two of them together, was extremely moved. He could see why Jesus favored them, as they exuded joy. He knew they had been hiding in the bushes and they had witnessed him rescuing St. Peter. Always considerate of another's feelings, Wendy and Jillian did not want to embarrass St. Peter by acknowledging they had seen his precarious predicament. In fact, there were many qualities that would make them the ideal candidates for this task. Since the meeting, St. Michael had searched his heart and realized it was his intense fondness for the two of them which had caused him to be so opposed to this idea in the first place. But like any good angel, St. Michael knew he now needed to put his personal feelings aside. He now needed to do whatever he could to support the Father's wishes. He would do everything in his power to protect and guide them.

"Jesus told me He and Joy would soon be speaking to the two of you regarding His idea," St. Michael prompted. "At first, I thought it quite ridiculous but after some thought I think it could work. What do you think?"

Wendy and Jillian realized Jesus had already mentioned their names to St. Michael. Only having just discussed this with Jesus they were not certain how to respond.

"Jesus told me that He was considering the two of you for this assignment," continued St. Michael. "It is a most unusual assignment. I would think it would require careful consideration before volunteering. While it would seem very exciting on the surface, there would be many challenges and many choices afforded this angel; choices they had not been exposed to before. It would take an angel who had a great deal of tenacity and fortitude to even consider such an undertaking. The biggest challenge I can see is that an *earth angel* will be given the gift of free will. This could be a most interesting dilemma, especially for an angel who already sees free will as an easy thing to keep in check."

Wendy knew St. Michael was referring to her and Jillian. It is true they did have a difficult time understanding why human beings would exercise this free will to the exclusion of accomplishing their purpose. Wendy felt St. Michael thought the two of them naïve in this regard and as a result they oversimplified situations. Yes, until one experienced the gift of free will one could never really know what they would do.

"I quite agree, St. Michael," Wendy affirmed. "I know I have been critical of humans in the past. I know as angels we only desire to do that which is the will of our Father, but I think humans would desire to do so also if they could understand the true meaning of life. I know as time progresses they have no recollection from where they came but surely, they can be taught. I think to be an *earth angel* would be no easy task. That is for certain. I can only say for myself if I were to go I would do all I could to teach others about joy. I would do my best to accomplish what I was sent to do."

Jillian admired her sister's enthusiasm. She wished that she were not so skeptical, yet she felt if anyone could succeed at this it would be Wendy.

"You know, St. Michael, I admire Wendy for wanting to do this," Jillian added. "I wish I shared the same enthusiasm. There is a part of me that thinks this could really work. I have to say perhaps I am more selfish as I love being an angel. I cannot imagine what it would be like to not be in our Father's kingdom. I can't imagine what it would be like to be asked to believe sight unseen in His kingdom. It must be very difficult. I am sure St. Peter can attest to that?"

"Yes, my little one. There is much that is asked for the gift of free will in return," St Michael responded. "Humans must rely on their faith, a faith which is tested time and time again. Although, it is a part of the life process, it can be most disheartening for those who do not succeed. It is very easy to get distracted because there are so many distractions not of God on earth. More and more Satan is using tactics which humans are not recognizing as his. Not to cast a shadow on this experiment but it is important that whoever attempts this see the challenges which lie ahead! I think the two of you are model examples of joy in our Father's kingdom, but you must remember here you are protected. You only know what is of the Father. Certainly, you are aware of Lucifer and his tribe of fallen angels, but you have never done battle with Lucifer without your heavenly armor. Such is not the case for humans. Humans must rely upon the **Holy Spirit** to guide and protect them. Many do not acknowledge the existence of Lucifer and therefore do not seek what is of the spirit. Yes, whoever attempts this will be sorely tested."

"I am so glad we ran into the two of you today," said Wendy. "There is so much to think about and I will consider everything you have said. I know, St. Michael, I was not the best guardian angel. I also know many in the kingdom think we are naïve. Maybe those qualities which made us not the best of guardians might in some way be valuable as *earth angels*. My, we have talked so long standing in the sun here, St. Peter. Your wings are almost dry."

"Yes, you must have had quite a swim!" chimed Jillian. Wendy and Jillian both knew there was much to be considered and they would need time to think about what had been discussed. Therefore, it was not a surprise to St. Peter or St. Michael they were changing the subject.

"Yes, you are quite right, I am almost dried out now," replied St. Peter. "That reminds me it is time for us to get back." While they would liked to have stayed and talked with them some more, they were being summoned by the Angel of Peace. These days it was rare if angels of their status had time to indulge in any sort of lengthy conversation.

Wendy and Jillian knew they had been given a gift. There were not many in the Father's kingdom who had shared such a conversation with both St. Michael and St. Peter, for they truly were the highest on the angelic realm and as a result were kept very busy. Wendy and Jillian thought it was quite a coincidence the four of them ran into each other. In retrospect, Wendy and Jillian had never seen St. Peter and St. Michael swimming there before, at least not when they were there. However, in the Father's kingdom, there truly is no such thing as a coincidence, as humans refer to on earth.

Yes, St. Michael and St. Peter had planned to visit with the two of them and Wendy and Jillian knew they should think long and hard about what was to come. Each knew the seriousness of these times and that something had to be done; something that would help prepare God's children for the trials and tribulations that would soon befall the earth.

Chapter 2

Wendy

Wendy felt she was more than ready for her assignment. The Angel of Joy had spent countless hours detailing what she felt was most pertinent for her to know in preparation for this most unusual assignment. What she was not ready for was the vast darkness she now found herself surrounded by. Even though the Angel of Joy had told her it was just a temporary condition it was a most foreign condition, indeed. Wendy was so used to the illuminating lightness in her Father's kingdom she was not at all prepared for the darkness she was now encountering. For this reason the Father had seen to it she would still be able to communicate with her beloved sister as well as the Angel of Joy. Actually, Joy was going to use this time to mentor Wendy on all she would need to remember during her stay on earth. This information would be deeply imbedded in the recesses of her soul. The Angel of Joy worried Wendy would be under severe attack while on earth and wanted to make certain Wendy would be able to guard herself against the mighty attacks of Satan. Joy was all too familiar with the many tools he used to lure away God's chosen people.

Although she was certain Satan had no idea of the Father's latest plan, she knew it was just a matter of time before He heard of what Jesus was planning.

"Wendy, you must understand, as an *earth angel*, you will experience free will and as a result you will be able to fully understand the temptations and emotion humans experience," said Joy. "Even though you do not think this can happen because you are so filled with love and enthusiasm for our heavenly Father, you will be distracted many times over the course of your lifetime. Even you, I am afraid, will have periods of time when you will lose sight of what truly matters! But I tell you Wendy, you will not fail! There will be times you are greatly discouraged, yet our Father and I will always be there for you."

These were the words Wendy would mull over time and time again while waiting for her earthly arrival. She needed to remember she was a part of her Father's great plan and that she was the first to be chosen for such an assignment. For this very reason she knew she could not fail. There were many who were looking to her to succeed, to lead the way for others to follow. As an *earth angel* she was assured she would be given the tools she needed in order to complete her assignment.

She also was assured Jillian would meet up with her at the appropriate time to help her accomplish her mission. Together they would accomplish much. As *earth angels* they would be able to go and teach where ministers and people of the cloth could not go, hence their success would not be measured by the standards of man, but by the Father, himself. They would know when to relinquish free will and as a result, would then choose to do what the Father had called them to do. Wendy could not imagine having difficulty relinquishing free will as she had yet to experience this so called freedom.

Little did Wendy understand that free will would help her formulate her own lesson plan on earth. By the time Wendy and Jillian would reunite they would both have acquired sufficient knowledge to complete what the Father was preparing them to do. Until she saw her beloved Jillian again, Wendy would not remember her heavenly origin nor would she remember the reason she had been brought to earth. She would have no idea she was an *earth angel*, a soldier in the almighty army of God chosen to arrive at this particular time.

Wendy and Jillian knew this would be no easy assignment, yet Joy reassured them saying, "I have seen your strength and know in the end the two of you will be faithful to our Father. These are crucial times. You must listen to the still voice inside you for it is this still voice that will show you who you are, where you are to go and what you are to do. You must learn to be *sly as a serpent and innocent as a dove* and, my dear Wendy, always remember you are among His chosen people. When you least expect it you and Jillian will have a personal encounter with Jesus. He will come to you in a manner the two of you, as humans, can and will accept."

If not for her conversations with Joy, Wendy feared she would have asked to be reassigned, not that it would have done any good. The Father had told her once she embarked on this journey she would not be allowed to change her mind. It was just a matter of days before she would be brought out of this darkness and into the light. However, she was not prepared for what was to follow.

Wendy knew something was about to change as the safe haven in which she had been sheltered in for the past nine months became turbulent. It was as if some convulsive force was thrusting her closer and closer to an unforeseen opening, which with each thrust became larger and larger. Although she knew this was the birth canal they had talked about, Wendy had little idea birth would be such an ordeal, not to mention her earthly mother seemed, for an instant, most discomforted with her arrival. Never had Wendy heard such screams! Jesus had told her what a gift a new born baby was to its mother, yet judging from the screams of torment her new mother was making Wendy wondered if she had misunderstood what Jesus had said. In fact these screams were definitely causing her to reconsider her assignment. Maybe it would be best to resign! Just as she was sending up these very same thoughts to her Father in heaven Wendy felt her first connection with another human being.

Wow, these humans were something else! Why was she being treated in such a manner? Not only was her mother crying (thank heavens quietly) but the man in white was holding her upside down and slapping her on her delicate behind. Wow, no one had ever told her the beginning of human life was quite like this! No wonder so many humans had such a difficult time on their journey in life, if this was any indication of how things started.

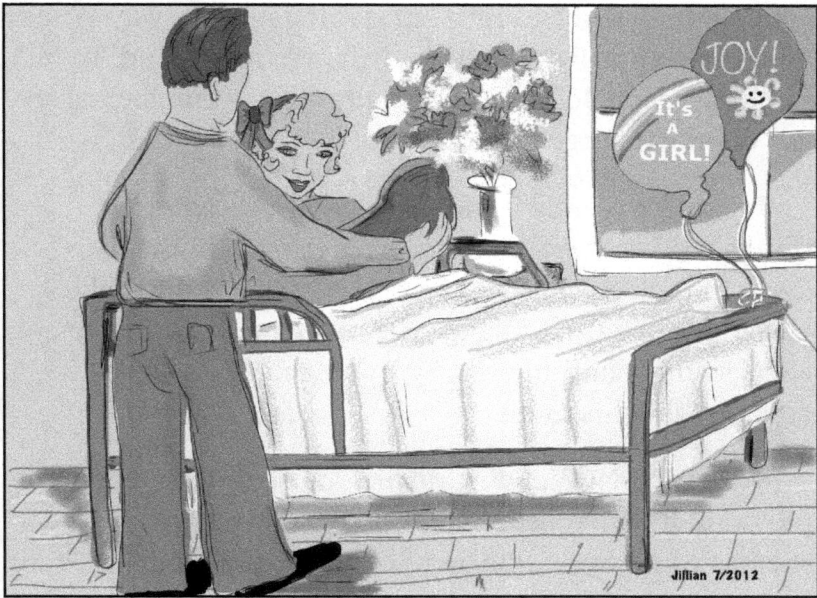

Jillian 7/2012

Just when Wendy thought things were never going to turn around she was placed gently in her mother's arms. Except for the love in Jesus' eyes, she had never experienced such a warm and loving look as her new mother was adorning her with. There were other people in the room as well and they all seemed to be talking and laughing at once. She was delighted to know she was now the source of much attention and seemed to be bringing much joy to all concerned. It was just as Joy had said it would be; quite a joyous occasion after all. What seemed like just a few seconds to Wendy had been quite a lengthy ordeal, as her reluctance to arrive caused a great deal of discomfort for Wendy's new mother.

Joy said it took a lot of convincing to get Wendy to forge ahead as she wanted to go back from where she had come. She said she found it most amusing the way Wendy kept telling our Father she had changed her mind. In fact, the Father and Joy had to do quite a bit of convincing to get Wendy to forge ahead.

Joy said, "Wendy is happy to know everyone thinks she is cute, although a little lacking in the hair department." According to her new father, "What she lacked for in hair,' he said," she made up for with her rosy cheeks and beautiful eyes." Wow, Wendy thinks she is going to like this man!

So there it is; Wendy's auspicious beginning. It is as they said it would be. She has no recollection of where she has come from. She loves being human and feels very lucky to have the parents she has. As a child she naturally feels close to Jesus. Everything is such an adventure for her and as many children do, Wendy thought the world was her playground.

Joy watched Wendy the very first time she truly noticed a cloud. She was just certain it was made of cotton candy and if Wendy tried really hard she could get hold of it. When she found out it was not reachable Wendy was most distraught. However, it did not take her long to come to understand the magnitude of her imagination and it wasn't long before she would imagine herself jumping in the center of these billowy clouds. In short, as a child she never doubted the world was indeed her playground.

Wendy loved flowers and all that nature had to offer. As a child there was hardly a flower she did not smell. One particular time when she was sniffing her aunt's yellow lilies, she had a recollection of a sweet smell she had experienced somewhere in the recesses of her past. She just couldn't get enough of them. When Wendy went into the bathroom and looked in the mirror there was a big yellow spot on the end of her nose. She was so frightened! Wendy went running out to her mother who burst out laughing when she saw her. Seeing her distress her mother quickly assured her it was simply the pollen from the flower she had smelled, which had somehow left its mark on the tip of her nose. She also said it was her guardian angel's way of showing her she had just been kissed by a heavenly being.

This was the beginning of quite a conversation about guardian angels. Her mother said it was as if she couldn't get enough information about them. It was then she knew she had her very own guardian angel and in the future would spend many countless hours talking to her angel. She was her playmate. Sometimes she would talk to her out loud. It wasn't until she became much older that Wendy confined these conversations to a much quieter nature. Over time she began to spend less and less time with her guardian. This doesn't mean she went anywhere, for in truth it was Wendy who let go. This is always hard on guardian angels as they love their humans so. When one is young they are so fresh and so innocent. In point of fact, when one is young they are so close to the Divine. Everything seems to hold such wonder and magic. It is only as one becomes more involved in the world they begin to distance themselves from our heavenly Father. At some point even Wendy, an *earth angel*, stopped looking at the world through the eyes of a child.

Some of her friends go to church every weekend. This is not the case with Wendy's family. She doesn't know why this is as she loves Jesus so and her parents say they love Him too. Maybe the problem is they cannot decide on which church to attend. They have gone to so many different churches over the years. Her parents pray, yet they don't talk about Him like Wendy does. In fact, a lot of people don't talk about Jesus like Wendy does. She can't say she understands why this is, it just is. Many times she would go to church by herself. She would go to the service rather than Sunday school as she loved to look at the statues; all except the one where Jesus is nailed on the cross. This one makes her cry as she finds it very sad anyone would hurt the Jesus whom she loves so very much. She can't understand why anyone would want to do such a thing to her beloved Jesus. Personally, she would never hurt anyone and therefore is convinced the world is a good place. Wendy's certain man is intrinsically good, is he not?

Her mother and father say she is a very sweet child. In fact, one time Wendy overheard her mother telling her aunt what a good child she was, what a special child she was. She said it was a wonder God hadn't taken her away as she had been quite sickly as a child. Of course, after hearing that, she wasn't so certain she wanted to be quite so good any more.

If one more person comments on how sweet she is Wendy is going to cry. She is looking at the comments in her High School annual now and cannot believe how many of her friends say the same identical thing! She finds herself wishing they would use some other adjective. What's wrong with being cool, hip, pretty, just anything rather than sweet! Sweet sounds so outdated, it sounds so corny. What is so great about being sweet anyway?

To Wendy It seems as though her childhood has flown by. Soon, she will be graduating. Although she has never been a great student, all of the ideas of what she would like to become would require more education. Not to mention, she has not received much encouragement for vocations in which she expressed an interest in. The only thing she has ever truly desired to do is to work for our Father. Wendy considered three different vocations; a minister, a nun and a social worker. Because her parents were not religious she was discouraged from the first two and as far as becoming a social worker was concerned, her mother felt Wendy's heart was too soft. She felt she would never be able to cope with the suffering she would see. Since the only thing Wendy has ever truly desired to do is work for our Father and no one thinks her capable of attaining her goals, perhaps, she is meant to simply get married and raise a family. And so her aspirations were deterred. It is a good thing to want to be married and have a family or is it not?

Wendy still listens to the still voice which comes from the center of her being but must admit her conversations with Jesus have grown less and less frequent over time, not to mention she doesn't even think about her guardian angel at all anymore.

"Why should I think of my angel anyway? Some guardian she is," thinks Wendy. "After all, look at how sick my earthly mother has become."

Wendy does talk to Jesus about her mother, the woman she has come to love so very much. However, now her mother is in a wheel chair and unable to walk. They say she has multiple sclerosis and has only two years to live. Wendy knows this is wrong. She knows this is an error. Jesus would never let something so tragic happen to her mother. No, that was not the Jesus that she knew and loved with all of her heart. Wendy is not angry with God as she knows her mother will get better. Wendy is confident He will answer her prayer. He does hear and does answer her prayers. Her mother lives! Her mother walks!

Wow, her mom is out of a wheel chair now and she is even putting on weight. She is such a positive person and everyone gives her so much credit for her recovery, yet she thinks Jesus deserves a little more recognition for her recovery. A lady called from somewhere (her mom never said where) and wanted her to talk about the miracle but Wendy's mother was afraid.

Wendy is thinking, "There must be more miracles that have happened and wonders why no one wants to talk about them? If they don't share how will anyone ever know Jesus is real and He is very much alive?"

Why at 19 is Wendy starting to get discouraged? She loves to laugh and loves to smile, yet as she walks down the streets this is not what she sees. It is Christmas, her favorite time of year and she doesn't see much joy on the faces around her.

"How could this be?" she wonders, "The world is such a beautiful place! Perhaps, I am blinded by my love for

Jesus. Perhaps, it is true I am too sweet. Maybe it is I who need to change? In the end it is I who need to conform to the standards of man. What kind of standards can these be when there seems to be so little joy? Wendy decides she needs to toughen up after all she is all grown up now and out of school.

Wendy still doesn't attend any particular church. However, she does love Jesus, and still wants to do what is kind and what is good. Somehow, Wendy doesn't feel so good any more. Many of her dreams and aspirations don't seem possible. Actually, she doesn't remember too many people giving Jesus credit for healing her mother.

St. Michael and the Angel of Joy had been keeping a close watch over Wendy over the years. There were many times they wished Wendy could sense their presence. It was so hard to watch her witness firsthand the trials and tribulations of the world, yet they were quite pleased with her progress to date. She had remained most steadfast in her faith as Jesus said she would. Although she could not fully understand the depth or meaning of her feeling for the Divine, she was most receptive to the promptings of her soul. She had of course, as an *earth angel*, been given the gift of discernment. She was able to listen to the still voice which comes from the center of one's being but lately they had both noticed she was becoming more and more distracted. She was not spending the time she needed in prayer to understand the Father's will for her. It was as if she were searching for her own human identity. Where was she to fit in this most complex world? Where would she find her security?

The angels knew because she was not given much encouragement by her earthly parents, Wendy was having a difficult time. Because she wasn't encouraged to follow her heart's desire, to work for Jesus, Wendy was now looking in a different direction. How could this be good? How could this allow Wendy to fulfill her calling? The direction she was now seeking would take her on an entirely different course than what they had anticipated in the beginning. Perhaps this was necessary. It was certainly not what they would have chosen for their beloved Wendy! When St. Michael and the Angel of Joy expressed their concerns to Jesus He simply smiled and said what He is famous for saying, *"Have faith My cherished ones!"*

Angels and humans alike are equipped with their own special gifts and talents. St. Michael and the Angel of Joy knew Wendy would not have been sent on this assignment without the necessary gifts to accomplish her mission. No, she would be given the very tools she would need in order to succeed. As a matter of fact, all *earth angels* are equipped with similar qualities. They exude strength and stand for justice. Their gentle presence radiates compassion and joy. They are tolerant of others while readily sharing their own gifts and talents with others.

Wendy would have the ability to see the good in everyone. She would have an endurance that most would not have. Jesus made certain all of His chosen people were well prepared for what was to come. Jesus would see to it Wendy would never become subject to the spirit of bitterness. He knew full well bitterness was one of Satan's tools. Jesus knew Wendy and His *earth angels* would need a strong sense of forgiveness.

In the beginning Jesus had given His word; He would not let her fail. She would have what she needed when she needed it. Although there would be many times she would become discouraged, He would never leave her side. She need only continue to listen and believe. The problem was St. Michael and the Angel of Joy knew she was not listening. Although her faith was strong it seemed Wendy was choosing free will over what was of her heavenly Father.

"Where is this man I am to spend the rest of my life with?" Wendy would pray. "Am I not destined to be a wife and a mother?" Night after night Wendy prayed the Lord would send to her the one she was to spend the rest of her life with. She was becoming most anxious and felt most alone. So many of her friends had married; it seemed there was no one there for Wendy. Certainly, Jesus would send someone to her soon. Wendy felt as though life was passing her by and did not understand what she was called to do. Yet, she sensed there was a deeper purpose for her life.

Perhaps, she was meant to join the Peace Corp? She decides to take an extra job to earn the money she needs to travel. Yes, this must be what she is called to do.

Then it happened, much as St. Michael and the Angel of Joy said it would; Wendy was falling for Richard, a customer of the bank where she worked. St. Michael and Joy knew Wendy would experience much sorrow if they were to be together. Yet, it was happening right in front of their very eyes. She was so infatuated with him and they were powerless to stop it.

They knew Wendy had been longing for marriage and even though she had been working towards joining the Peace Corp, she did not feel the enthusiasm required to follow through. Now it seemed as though this man, this Richard, was about to steal her heart. As sure as the sun rises in the morning, St. Michael had every right to be alarmed. Wendy was falling head over heels in love with Richard.

"Isn't there anything that we can do?" St. Michael inquired of Jesus.

"You already know the answer to that Michael," Jesus answered, *"If she comes to Me in prayer, I will warn her this is not in My will for her, yet in the end the decision must be hers."*

For a while it seemed as if St. Michael's and the Angel of Joy's prayers were to be answered. They knew Wendy was communing with the Father on this delicate subject. She came so close to listening, to obeying what the Father was telling her to do, yet in the end she could not send Richard away.

And so what was for Wendy a most joyous occasion brought great sadness to her two beloved guardians. They knew all too well what was in store for Wendy. Would this not break her spirit, altogether? She was such a good person and possessed an innocence which was part and parcel of the characteristics of an *earth angel*.

Wendy was about to embark upon a journey from which there was no turning back. Oh, if only she had truly heeded the Father's warning. So much sadness could have been avoided, of that they were certain.

Wendy had always wanted a large family and was certain this would come in time. She and Richard already had one child and she felt it was just a matter of time before they had another, after all she had told Richard prior to marriage she wanted to have five children. Since he didn't disagree she was confident her dream would come true. Four years had passed since their son's arrival and there still was no mention of when they could have another child. Wendy soon was to find out firsthand why her heavenly Father did not want them to marry. She would come to understand the consequences of not listening to her beloved Father, as the Father knows the true measure of each of His children's hearts. He knew full well the state of Richard's heart. Richard did not have a relationship with Jesus and therefore was easily influenced by the longings of the flesh.

Jesus had warned Wendy this was not the relationship for her. He had told her they were not equally yoked, yet she had refused to listen to the still voice which comes from within. It was not that she did not hear. Each person, *earth angel* or not, has the ability to hear what the Father is saying. Yet, when so many do not get the answer they desire, they pretend not to have heard; they ignore that which they know to be true. They do not listen to the longings and the calling of the soul.

"Through sorrow comes Joy!" Jesus exclaimed. *"You must not let this get you down, Joy. You must have faith when the time comes, when the time is right, Wendy will know that which she is called to do. For I tell you, she will be protected. She will learn many lessons as a result of this relationship. In the end she will draw once again to Me. I will send her the people she needs to help her during this most difficult period of her life, so you must be patient now and know I will not allow her to experience more than she can bear. In the weeks and months to come she will come to know the truth. She will see the light once again and know she is a child of God."*

Wendy could not believe this was happening. Had she not been a good wife? Had she not been a good mother? What on earth had she done to warrant what was happening? Why would God let this happen? How could Jesus allow Richard to leave them? How could Richard fall in love with another woman? This couldn't be happening to them. No, Jesus would not allow this. He would make everything better, of this she was convinced. Hadn't she been faithful?

This was the beginning of a nightmare from which Wendy could not awaken. The day Richard moved out was a day like none other. What human being could do this to his family? What kind of father would desert his children? "What did I do?" Wendy cried. Richard explained it was nothing she had done. He simply said he was not a family man and since the arrival of their second child knew he was not cut out for this type of life. He assured her she had been a model wife and mother. The problem was with him not with her.

"You've got that one right, buddy!" St. Michael exclaimed. It was tearing his heart apart to watch as Wendy rocked back and forth in disbelief and despair. He wanted to whisk her back to the gates of heaven. This had gone far enough as far as he was concerned. If it was up to him he would give Richard a lesson he would never forget! Yet, St. Michael knew he would not be allowed to intervene. Sometimes it was extremely difficult being a guardian of humans!

Chapter 3

Jillian

Joy knew all too well the feelings Jillian was now having regarding the loss of her soul sister. Although they would meet up again at a later date, Joy could sense the magnitude of Jillian's sadness. At first Jillian was most indignant Wendy had made the decision to leave, for in truth Wendy and Jillian had never been separated. Jillian could not understand why Wendy would want to leave their heavenly realm; for the two of them had experienced firsthand, as the guardians of humans, the trouble free will could get one into. She also knew how much Wendy scorned the so called "gift of free will" and wondered how Wendy would react to the human condition. Jillian had always felt very protective towards Wendy. Many times as a guardian Wendy would ignore the rules of guardianship. Had it not been for Wendy ignoring these rules, she and Wendy would not have been removed from their role as guardians and become guardians of the little cherubs. Perhaps, if they had still been in the role of earthly guardians, Wendy would not have volunteered for this dangerous assignment.

Although Jillian knew there was no point in crying over Wendy going to earth, she simply could not wrap her wings around why Wendy would want to leave her and the little cherubs like this. Jillian had tried to convince Wendy to change her mind for hadn't Jesus told her she was free to do so? Even now at this late date Wendy could simply tell Jesus she didn't think she was up for the job. Yet, Jillian knew Wendy would never do anything to disappoint their Father, as Jillian felt the same way.

An angel loves their heavenly Father with all of their being and only desires to do that which is in his will. No angel would intentionally do anything to displease Him or the elders for that matter. Jillian remembered far too well the look on Jesus' face when he heard St. Michael had decided to remove them permanently as guardians of humans. Although Jesus was most kind when he summoned the two of them to discuss the matter, both Wendy and Jillian wished they could avoid what was sure to be a most uncomfortable meeting. Jillian would never forget how Wendy's wings fluttered as they stood in front of their beloved Father. Wendy had assured Jillian she would tell Jesus the latest debacle was her idea and to go easy on Jillian, but just as Wendy was about to confess she was the one who broke the rules, it was Jillian who took the blame before Wendy could even open her mouth! Wendy tried to tell Jesus not to believe Jillian but Jesus had already made up his mind. Due to their childlike antics they would now be reassigned as guardians of the heavenly cherubs. Although Jesus was most disconcerted to hear of their earthly antics, He truly loved the two of them and sincerely thought this shift in assignments would benefit all.

Hadn't their reassignment taught Wendy a lesson? How could she possibly expose herself to this difficult new assignment? Jillian held out hope Wendy would come to her senses over time. Even if Wendy didn't come to her senses, perhaps, St. Michael would intervene for surely he had seen firsthand the trouble Wendy had gotten the two of them into before. Yet, here it was the day before Wendy was to leave her heavenly abode and it seemed there was nothing to do but say goodbye. Jillian now regretted the time she had spent being angry at Wendy, for in truth she was simply trying to protect her sister. She just didn't see how Wendy could manage without her. However, deep down Jillian did not see how she could get along without her beloved friend. The Angel of Joy had told Jillian she would give her updates on how Wendy was doing over time, yet somehow Jillian knew she would never truly be at peace until the two of them were reunited. What Wendy could not know was that Jillian's love for her would be the catalyst in Jillian's decision to join Wendy, in this most important assignment. Jesus never doubted Jillian would volunteer for the task. He and He alone knew the measure of love the two of them held for one another. Jesus knew it was just a matter of time before Jillian would come to Him and ask to join her sister in this most important assignment.

One must recall heavenly time is not the same as on earth. In earthly time it was to be years before Jillian would summon the courage to make this life-changing decision. Jillian had never wanted to experience the human condition in the way Wendy had. She was more than content in her ethereal status and loved being guardian of the cherubs, yet since Wendy had left, nothing seemed the same. Jillian spent a great deal of time worrying about Wendy. She had heard rumors of what was to come in the world and as a result was beginning to understand the importance an *earth angel* would play in the not too distant future. Yes, she needed to be with Wendy. They would stand side by side in this critical battle.

Jillian was prepared for her role as an *earth angel*, for she had been schooled in the art of joy, as well. She and Wendy had been taught by the best and Jillian felt comfortable in the knowledge she had attained. When Jesus told the Angel of Joy about Jillian's decision, her reaction was one of relief. She had watched Jillian over the years and knew her heart was with her beloved sister. She did not try to discourage Jillian because she still remembered the look on Jillian's face the day Wendy left for her earthly assignment.

All that was necessary was for the details to be worked out. Due to earthly circumstances it would not be possible for Jillian to be part of the same family as Wendy. In truth, Jillian would need to experience a more religious background which would provide valuable insight for the two of them. While Jillian was most anxious to be rejoined with her sister, she understood this could not occur until Jesus felt the time was right. In the meantime, she was to exercise the gift of free will in making choices that would help her learn the lessons she would need for her undertaking. Jesus knew when the time would be right for the two of them to come together. Each of them

would need to experience firsthand the consequences
of the choices they made, for these lessons would prove
valuable in their assignment. Wendy and Jillian would
embark on different roads before their paths would cross.
It would be more than thirty earth years before Wendy
and Jillian would meet. Jesus wanted each to learn
important skills and lessons before they were reunited.

Many in the heavens were anxiously waiting for this
moment in time. St. Michael and the Angel of Joy knew
what was in store for Wendy and Jillian. Once Wendy and
Jillian were reunited, Jesus would spend a great deal of
time with them, as nothing could be left to chance. They
would need to be refreshed in the art of joy-filled living.
They would know they worked for the Father. He would
remind them of their purpose on earth. He would see to
it they would lead His children to the "cave within". This
cave within would be a "safe haven" for Jesus' weary trav-
elers. It is in this haven man would commune with their
heavenly Father. This would be where all would come to
find the answers they would seek!

Jillian was anxious to join her beloved sister, Wendy.
Although the Angel of Joy had been giving her weekly
updates on Wendy's progress, she knew in her heart the
sooner she arrived on earth the sooner she and Wendy
would be reunited. She missed the times they had spent
floating side by side on the azure waters. She missed
Wendy's sense of humor and longed to hear her sister's
magical laughter, for when Wendy and Jillian laughed
together the entire kingdom could hear them from miles
away. Many times the little cherubs would ask Jillian

to relive the adventures she and Wendy had shared as guardian angels. These stories entertained the little ones so, yet they caused Jillian to become increasingly anxious to get on with her earthly assignment. Jillian knew all too well what was to come. She knew all too well the adversities each would need to overcome before they would be reunited.

Jillian knew once she arrived on earth more than 30 years would pass before they would see one another again. Although earthly time is but a blink of an eye in heaven, these years could seem like an eternity for human beings. The Angel of Joy reminded Jillian of this fact a little too often as far as Jillian was concerned. She knew Joy was trying to protect her, yet all she did was add to Jillian's growing restlessness. When the day had finally come for Jillian's departure many in the heavens came to bid her farewell.

St. Michael and St. Peter were there along with her beloved mentor, Joy. Jesus would see to the final details and so she would feel His holy presence as each step progressed. She knew this would be the last time for a very long time she would actually be able to see her beloved friends face to face, for once her journey began she knew they would no longer be visible to her.

St. Michael had assured Jillian he would watch over her throughout the duration of her earthly journey and that no harm would come to either her or Wendy. The Angel of Joy would communicate with Jillian as long as she would acknowledge her. Yet, the Angel of Joy knew there would come a time when Jillian would no longer

talk to her guardian angel; for the rigors of life would distract her from heavenly thoughts. Nonetheless, the Angel of Joy would act as Jillian's guardian angel just as she had been and would continue to be for Wendy.

It had been decided Jillian would be born into a family which was well schooled in religion. Specifically, she was to be reared in the Catholic faith, providing a good balance for Wendy who was not reared in any particular religion. The two of them each loved Jesus with all of their heart. This love for their beloved Jesus was natural, as He was intrinsically part and parcel of each of their being. Many years would pass before the two of them would realize most humans did not share this intense love of Jesus. Many humans did not acknowledge Him at all. Unlike Wendy, Jillian attended church on a regular basis with her family. Most family parties were in celebration of religious holidays. Jillian's mother and grandmother were devout Catholics who practiced their faith daily. They taught Jillian and her siblings about the Angels and Saints and the Ten Commandments. Jillian attended Catholic school as a child and therefore, was well versed in the inner workings of the church. She was also taught about the protection specific saints could provide.

Jillian was always surrounded by statues of the Holy Family. She was taught the importance of the Blessed Mother and other angels. For Jillian it seemed as though Jesus and her heavenly Family were always around, she never doubted their existence. Of course, if the truth be told, Jillian's great faith in Jesus had been instilled in her long before her arrival on earth, just as Wendy's had.

St. Michael was most impressed by Jillian's religious upbringing. He could now understand why each of their earthly backgrounds needed to be so very different. While Wendy was raised in a secular environment she had always been very close to the Holy Family. Jillian would be able to teach Wendy about the inner workings of the Church and Wendy would be able to share her unquestioning relationship with Jesus. Each in their own way considered Jesus their true Father and knew He was the reality and not the illusion, as so many humans believed.

One might compare Jillian to Joan of Arc, for even as a small child Jillian would stand up passionately for her beliefs, never compromising her values or principles, as some of her peers did. Jillian was equipped with a strong faith and never doubted what she knew to be true. Over the

years Jillian would rely on this faith when making pivotal changes along her life's journey.

Although there were some major differences in their upbringings there also were surprising similarities. Both

Wendy and Jillian's mothers suffered from ill health throughout their lives. Wendy spent much time conversing with Jesus, petitioning Him for a miraculous healing. Wendy was a quiet child and, much the same as Jillian, never caused any trouble for her earthly parents. They were both filled with the goodness of the Holy Spirit and only wanted intrinsically to complete their earthly mission, even if they hadn't yet discovered it. So, while Jillian exemplified the traits and strengths of Joan of Arc, those who knew Wendy saw her characteristics to personify those cultivated by St. Francis of Assisi. While Jillian was confrontational; Wendy reflected quietly on spiritual matters. Yes, some day they would make a fine team, indeed!

Jesus had planned very well. He knew the knowledge each would obtain along their journey would provide them with the necessary tools they would use together when the time was right. Whatever they had not learned by the time they were reunited they would learn from the Angel of Joy and Jesus, Himself. Nothing in the future would be left to chance. Jesus had formed a covenant with each of them from the beginning. He had made certain each could feel His presence in all things as this was crucial for their survival and success.

Jillian knew without a shadow of a doubt she would always work for the Lord in some capacity. Neither she nor Wendy would understand until they were reunited what that capacity would be. They were drawn to one another like magnets, for at a soul level they knew each other well. By the time Wendy and Jillian met again, each would have learned about free will through trial and error. Soon, they would only desire to do the Father's will knowing this was the work they were destined to do. This was the work they would carry out in their assignments as *earth angels*!

Chapter 4

The Reunion

The Angel of Joy and Saint Michael were on pins and needles waiting for the precise moment Wendy and Jillian were to be reunited on earth. Although they would have no prior knowledge of having been together before, each would recognize something familiar in the other. Although each had come from distinctly different backgrounds they would soon find they had much in common with one another. In earth years they would be ten years apart, which in heavenly time was but a fleeting moment.

As previously planned by the Father, each of their careers was in the banking industry. Even though they lived in different cities Jesus knew at the appropriate time they would be reunited. Their careers were simply to be the platform for this reunion.

The Angel of Joy was spending a great deal of time with each of them now. Although she was not allowed to intercede with the choices they made, once acted upon, she was however, able to gently nudge each of them in the right direction. She knew once they came together there would be much that would need to happen in order to prepare them for what they had been sent to earth to accomplish.

Wendy had become increasingly restless of late and was having a difficult time understanding why this was. Her career had never been more promising having far exceeded her assigned goals. As a result, she had received numerous awards for her performance and was compensated accordingly. Even though she had worked very hard to arrive at this stage in her career she was now questioning the direction her life had taken.

Wendy loved Jesus as much as ever and felt there had to be a deeper purpose for her life. Yet, she was unsure as to what road, if any, she should take at this time. She loved to motivate others and held a deep appreciation for one another's gifts. Wendy loved to help others achieve their potential and knew this potential could manifest itself in many different ways, other than that of one's immediate employment. Many times her mind would wander to that of a higher nature, to that of a higher purpose. Wendy wanted so much to help others to lead a richer more enlightened way of life. Of course little did she realize at this time these promptings were coming from the deepest part of her soul. And so it was no surprise to the Angel of Joy and St. Michael when Wendy decided to give notice on her job to entertain becoming a motivational speaker.

"This is perfect," exclaimed St. Michael. "Now, all we need to do it to get Jillian to apply for Wendy's old position so the two of them can meet!"

"Oh, St. Michael, that is no problem," Joy responded, "as Jillian has been just as restless, as of late, in her job and I have been encouraging her to spread her wings. As a matter of fact, she had an interview today with Wendy's boss and I have been advised, by the highest authority, he will offer her the position!"

"But how are they going to get to know each other if Wendy leaves the company?" asked St. Michael.

"Not to worry Michael as I will see to it Wendy has a change of heart. She will not leave the company until the appropriate time, of that you can be certain!"

Wendy was most anxious to meet her replacement, Jillian, as her boss had commented on how very much alike the two of them were. Her job now was to get Jillian settled into her new position and then she would be free to embark upon her new career.

The Angel of Joy knew time was of the essence and had to make certain Wendy would be convinced to stay and so it was no surprise to her when Wendy was called to meet with senior management.

Wendy truly did not want to fly to Seattle for this meeting, yet she felt out of courtesy she should at least listen to what they had to say, as she was fairly certain she would not have a change of heart. Of course, little did she know how strongly she was being guided now and so it was Wendy accepted another position within the company which would enable her to become close friends with Jillian. These were truly God incidences. Wendy

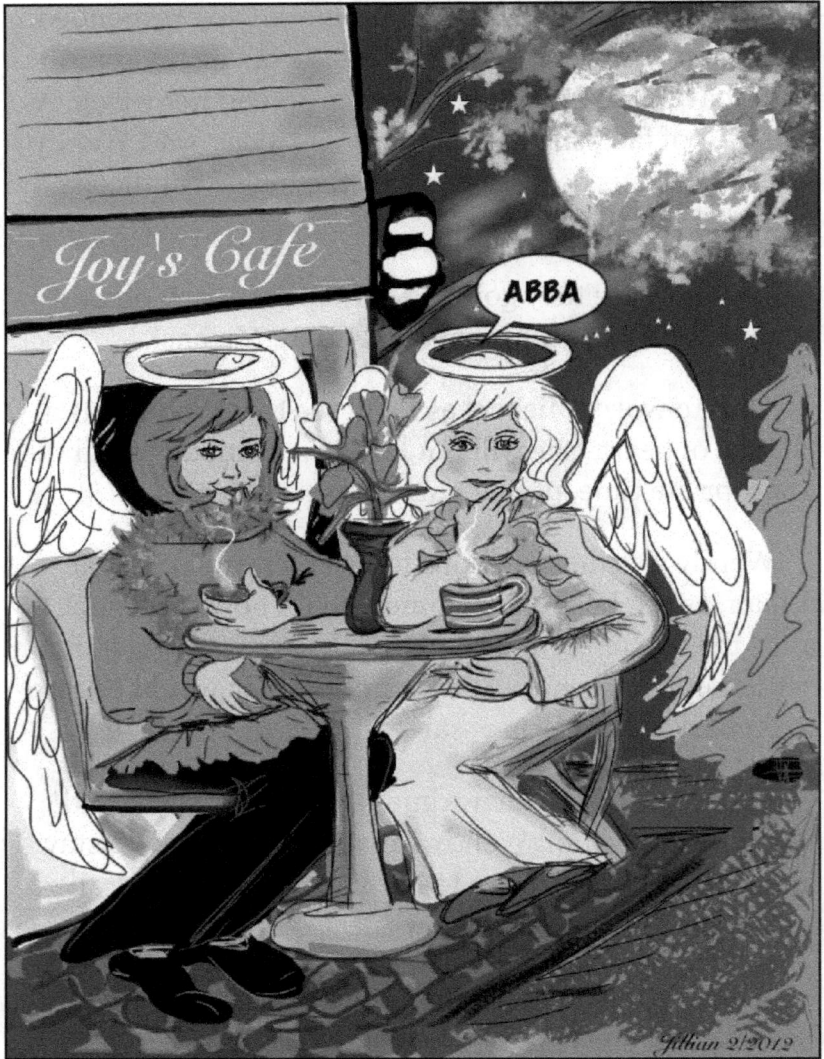

and Jillian became fast friends in the following months. Each of them expressed a strong desire to help others utilize their natural gifts and talents for the betterment of mankind. There were so many in these days who were caught up in the throes of materialism. As the days and weeks passed Wendy and Jillian understood they were kindred spirits and so it was only a matter of time before they would form a partnership. They were to embark now upon a journey which would be the beginning of their duties as *earth angels*.

And so it was they named their new found partnership ABBA and Company. In the secular world ABBA would stand for "A Better Business Alternative" and in the non-secular sense, would of course, stand for "The Father's Company".

The primary objective would be to teach others the art of joy-filled living. They would need to be sly as serpents in the workplace, for they would not be allowed to openly talk about God in this arena. While these were the most rewarding years of their lives their success was not appreciated by the standards of man. Little did they know these years would merely provide the training and experience for what was to come in the future. There would be much that would need to transpire before they would be able to truly accomplish their purpose. It would not be until much later each would understand they had not failed the mission their Father had sent them to accomplish.

Part 2

Part 2

Chapter 5

Satan Vs Angels

The angels in heaven were on full alert. They knew it was just a matter of time before they would be called to battle. Although they knew what had been foretold since the beginning of time, they could not believe it would soon come to pass. Jesus had told them to be on full alert now. St. Michael had been spending more time with his legion now than ever before. He knew all too well the tools Satan would use to bombard mankind with, in these final days.

The news media was heavily influenced by evil. Their babble would penetrate each American household. Fear was one of Satan's strongest tools and what better way to spread fear than through the media. St. Michael knew fear could render a mere human helpless. It could create such despondency in the heart. There would be no room for hope.

St. Michael knew more humans would be tempted to take their own lives. He remembered the Great

Depression and felt strongly mankind would respond in the same manner, as years before. The guardian angels were put on high alert and instructed to pay close attention to their human charges. They must do all in their power to help them understand the meaning of these times.

Human beings had been distracted by the temptations of the world far too long. Many were so deeply imbedded in their earthly possessions. They listened only to the longings of the ego and built their houses upon the sand. Soon the sand would shift and they would see their very foundation crumble beneath them. The chosen ones who had built their houses upon the rock would survive the storm that was to come because they would listen to what the Father was calling them to do. Many who did not know the Father would not take heed. They would not pay attention to the heart of the matter and would be easily deceived by the cunning of Satan and his army. Satan knew mankind's ego would keep those in power from coming to agreement in time. Soon, his plan would come to fruition; all he needed to do was wait.

The guardians were reporting to St. Michael daily now on the massive repossessions in the housing market. Many of the humans who were losing their homes should not have been granted the loans in the first place, as their incomes could not keep up with the adjustable payments. Families were being forced to let go of homes which should have provided warmth and security for their loved ones.

Because more and more people were heavily dependent on credit to manage their day to day living expenses, few had managed to save money for a rainy day. Any unexpected interruption in employment would be disastrous for they were not prepared to handle the loss in income.

People now were losing their jobs at a faster pace than ever before; as a result the whole economy was in a tail spin. Many were being tested and the angels knew without a doubt this was just the beginning.

There would be those who would rise above the circumstances. Those who knew the Father could rely upon Him to help them through these most difficult times. To say a person's faith would be tested is to put it mildly, as so many of the guardian's charges did not have a relationship with Jesus. Yes, there were those who knew of Him but far too many did not cultivate this most important relationship. Satan was certain mankind would listen to what was of the world. Soon, people would become complacent and settle for any answer that would allow them to maintain the lifestyle they had grown accustomed to.

St. Michael fully understood what was happening. Many were filled with fear and could not see how they could make a difference in the overall outcome of things. No, many would gladly look to those who were willing to solve the issues at hand, even if it meant compromising their values and overlooking the magnitude of corruption which was taking place.

Jesus knew there were those humans who were filled with greed and who did not consider themselves responsible for others; they wore cloaks of deception well. Many people who had money in retirement funds were now losing what they had worked all of their lives to amass.

The angels knew how easily financial security could be taken away. Many humans deceived themselves into thinking the more money they had, the more possessions they acquired, the more secure they would be. Now all were seeing how fragile this shallow security was. Of course Satan was on full alert; he knew many would blame the Father for not protecting them from wolf like opportunists. Many would not be able to rise above their despondency. They would not be able to connect with what was the heart of the matter or what was truly important. Peace, for these humans, would not come easily.

To the Angels, the truly sad part was this was just the beginning of the trials and tribulations many were not prepared for. They knew when times were the darkest people must be assured of their heavenly Father's presence.

There were so many Doubting Thomas's now. Church attendance was at an all time low. Many families did not teach their children about spiritual matters. How could children thrive if they did not even know of their heavenly Father? How could they be comforted if they did not know they could go to Him in times of trouble and He would provide them comfort?

The Angels were appalled to learn that children were no longer allowed to pray in school; for many this had been the only opportunity to learn about our heavenly Father. As a result, the moral fiber of the younger generation was sorely lacking a strong foundation.

Because their foundations were so weak, it was easy for them to partake in immoral behavior. Children were becoming sexually involved at a much younger age than in the past. Safe sex was not only being taught in the schools it was being practiced. Abortion was a big issue for parents who did not want to be saddled with a child who was a product of their teenager's sexual involvements. Promiscuity ran rampant over society.

Marital vows were often not taken seriously and as a result the divorce rate had been increasing at an alarming rate. Many now were living together, rather than marrying, fearful of committing themselves to what they now viewed as a failing institution. Yet, it was this very lack of commitment, this very lack of being able to weather the stormy times, which fostered this lackadaisical attitude. The angels often wondered, if one cannot commit in front of God, where does commitment lie? What does a human feel committed to if not the sanctity of marriage? Yet, who could blame them? In these troubled times who would want to knowingly set themselves up for almost certain failure?

Those who were married with families had such busy lifestyles. In most cases both parents in the United States needed to work, leaving very little quality family time. Many times the guardians complained as they saw their little cherubs fending for themselves, resulting in situations which could put them in danger. Often times

St Michael had to step in to circumvent what could have ended in utter disaster. If the parents could be there how much easier life would be for all concerned. And to make matters even worse the little ones did not even know of their dear Jesus. This saddened Jesus as He loved the little children so.

The Angel of Peace was growing increasingly anxious. She knew until Jesus returned to earth wars would continue to be waged, yet she knew the greatest of battles was still to come. Mankind had become so preoccupied with his immediate situation. He did not even recognize the harsh reality of terrorism. How could he not recognize terrorism after the World Trade Center was bombed?

The Angel of Peace was so distraught when the United States was attacked. She did her best to try to keep the World Trade Center from being bombed, yet she knew as long as evil existed there would always be these types of atrocities. So many innocent lives were taken needlessly on that day. For a short time Americans banned together; they expressed their allegiance to the flag and to God. She watched as President Bush reviewed the wreckage, knowing full well the anger he was experiencing at such a needless loss of humanity. This would be the primary focus of his presidency, vowing that all Americans would be safe no matter what the cost. And so she and St. Michael watched over the President as he put the wheels in motion to stamp out terrorism for good throughout the world. President Bush vowed he would see an end put to this type of tyranny. He set his sights on Iraq, having been assured by his advisors they had weapons of mass destruction.

While St. Michael could certainly understand why President Bush was intent on preventing another attack on the United States, he also knew the information the President had been given regarding these weapons was not correct. In the meantime many Americans died fighting a most unpopular war. So many Americans were caught up in their serendipity worlds. Many activists blamed Bush for a cause they at one time had much support for. How fickle humans can be.

St. Michael knew full well the dangers that lurked throughout the world. He knew firsthand the evil hearts of mankind. Many did not value human life. There were those who lacked a moral conscience; their only goal was to destroy human life. There were so many who did not feel threatened. There were so many who refused to see the effects of evil in the world.

Angels are peaceful by nature. The angels knew there would never be peace until Jesus returned to earth. They knew Satan needed to be destroyed once and for all. Yet, there were so many humans who did not understand they were in the midst of a war between good and evil. Evil had permeated their homeland and now had its tentacles fully entwined in the United States of America.

What a better way to destroy America than through what it was consumed by. Satan had planned well. The "fat cat" society of America was about to take a fall; a fall which would keep America even more distracted than in the past, affording Satan an opportune time to implement the next stage of the plan he had been putting together for quite some time now.

The Angel of Joy understood only too well the ways of Satan. She knew there were so many humans who did not understand the difference between joy and happiness. She watched as Wendy and Jillian tried so hard to teach what she had imbedded in their very souls. Having come from the angelic realm, Jillian and Wendy had a natural affinity for joy. For others to survive the challenges ahead they would need to understand the true essence of joy. These were the times Wendy and Jillian had been brought to earth for. All they had done previously was simply in preparation for what was to come.

No matter how hard the government would try to forestall economic disaster many would be severely affected. Many more would lose their jobs and as a result would eventually lose their homes, as well. Many in the world did not even know the magnitude, the truth, of what was lurking behind the scenes. Because there was so much corruption, mankind would not be able to undo the evil that had taken many decades to manifest.

St. Michael knew Wendy and Jillian were beginning to understand these were the times He was referring to. Long ago Jesus had told Wendy she would know when the time had come. She would know when the time was right. He could see the two of them were listening in the still of the night, a time humans are most receptive to what their heavenly Father is saying. *When humans desire to spend more time in prayer, God is tapping at the windows of their soul.* So it was in these times that not only were Wendy and Jillian listening more intently, but all of Jesus' chosen ones were listening more intently as well.

Jesus' chosen people would need to cultivate their communication with the heavenly Father more now than ever. Now, they would need to keep one foot in the heavenly realm and one on the earth. This is not always easy to do, for the longing to be in the Father's kingdom is so overwhelming at times, it can create great despondency in humans. All distractions now would have to be at a minimum at best. It is these very distractions which were one of the strongest tools in Satan's arsenal and could prevent them from achieving their earthly missions.

Jesus' chosen soldiers now needed to arm themselves. They needed to hone their listening skills so they could hear what the Father was calling them to do. There would be much deception during these times. Americans were only now beginning to understand the magnitude of deception which was responsible for such gross financial and moral decay.

Wendy and Jillian, therefore, must avail themselves to their heavenly Father. Even though they were of angelic descent, being human was challenging in these times. There was something to say about the human element. Even though humans may sense danger, they often choose not to listen to the still voice which comes from the center of their being. They fail to heed the warnings the Father and their guardian angels are trying to project. Thus, it took Wendy some time to accept these were the times she and Jillian were brought to earth for.

It is not surprising she was in denial. Wendy loved her earthly family very much. She did not want to see them endure what had been foretold since the beginning of time. She did not want to accept these times would indeed occur in their life span, yet every ounce of her being told her she must listen intently now. She must listen and obey now more than ever.

Another reason for her denial was of course she did not think she and Jillian had been successful after they were reunited, having for ten years, held seminars in the art of joy-filled living. She felt in many ways she had failed Jesus. It wasn't as if they hadn't tried. It wasn't as if they weren't listening, or was it? Perhaps in retrospect their ego allowed them to become discouraged. For in truth, how could anyone truly know the impact one human being had on another?

As these times became more and more turbulent, Wendy understood what they had done before when working for ABBA, merely afforded them time to learn and to practice what they would shortly be called to do.

The Angel of Joy was breathing a sigh of relief as she was becoming most concerned Wendy was not listening, yet she knew in the deepest part of her being, she had taught her well. She was certain Wendy and Jillian would understand what would soon implode in the United States.

There were so many in the heavens who were praying for Wendy and Jillian. They knew all too well the job that lay ahead, not only for Wendy and Jillian, but for all of Jesus' chosen ones. These chosen would be called upon to warn others of the evil which was permeating and threatening each and every being.

It would be up to the *earth angels* to lead others to this safe haven, to this cave within. It is here all will find the answers they seek. For what is of the world one will not be able to trust. Many humans will be sorely tested. As a result, Jesus knew, contrary to what Satan boasted, many would come to know the Father and would no longer cling to, or covet that which was of the world.

The beauty of our heavenly Father is He can and does make all things work for good. This is what the angels and the others were counting on as they knew the love the Father had for all of His children. They also knew He now was shoring up His army to save as many souls as possible.

St. Michael and his legion were growing increasingly concerned over the continuous development of nuclear weapons. They knew all too well the devastation they could cause. He also knew mankind in the end would turn to such weapons. Nothing made him angrier than the thought of so many innocent humans being destroyed as a result of man's brutality. Mankind had been fighting since the beginning of time. Many times St. Michael would console the Angel of Peace who saw so much destruction and devastation as a result of evil.

"St. Michael, I have seen so much warring. I have seen so much destruction," exclaimed the Angel of Peace. "I don't know how our heavenly Father can stand what He sees. It must hurt him so much to see the cruelty that exists in the world. It must anger Him to know Satan has done such a good job of spreading his darkness through-out. And now, with what is to come, Satan must certainly be gloating. He must think he is winning and that he will triumph in the end. It makes me so angry to think of his smug face and what he must be telling the others. Just look at America! Just look at how he has managed this incredible deception. There were so many who didn't have any idea this was coming. There were far too many who were distracted. There will be many who are hurt and there will be many, because they do not recognize evil, who will still be deceived in the end. They won't even realize it until many have lost so much. It saddens me because it doesn't have to be this way."

"I know what you mean, my friend," St. Michael responded. "There are many good people with good intentions but they are not focusing on what is truly most important now. Often, I watch as Americans involve themselves in situations of which they are not fully knowledgeable about. War is never a good thing, yet there are times when one must defend what is honorable; when one must protect the innocent. Such is the case with Israel. Too many Americans condemn Israel for protecting their country. How can they judge when they do not know what it feels like to have their country continually bombarded? Rather, they should spend their energy on helping solve the problems in America first. Then, they should pray for clarity and wisdom; too many act without the complete knowledge of the situation.

Many times I see humans listen to the sound of their own voices. They do not know how to listen to, or how to determine what is the true heart of the matter. It is not that they are not well intended. It is just that sometimes their intentions are not honorable. Yet, who am I to judge the measure of a man's heart? For in reality it is only our heavenly Father who knows the true measure of His children's heart. The truth is mankind is in for the biggest battle of all times. This will be the final battle between good and evil. Until mankind accepts this he will never be able to rid the world of war; he will never find peace."

"Oh, St. Michael, you are such a good friend," cried the Angel of Peace, "I know you see so much and I forget sometimes how painful this must all be for you as well. I know evil has to be allowed to get to the magnitude it does in order for Satan to be destroyed. Only then will mankind understand, firsthand, how evil has indeed infiltrated their lives. I am hopeful once they understand they will pay close attention to what our heavenly Father is telling them. Yet, I also know Satan is on full alert now as well and will be sending out his arsenal in full force!"

Jesus knew His angels were becoming increasingly anxious. He also knew many wished He would just put an end to Satan and his legion sooner rather than later. He knew there were still so many souls which needed to be saved. In truth, if Jesus had His way every one of His children would be spared. Each and every one of His children would come to know the Father and understand why they are here and from where they have come.

Jesus could not allow himself to become impatient. He could not allow His anger to cause Him to move too soon. He would need to rely on His chosen ones now more than ever before. He would see to it they had the tools they needed. He would insure each of his children was filled with the necessary enthusiasm for their calling. Jesus knew of their devotion to Him and He was certain they would answer His call.

He would take every adversity in a human's life as an opportunity to evaluate what was truly important. He would take these challenges, these setbacks and trials, as a prime opportunity to teach them what truly mattered. Often, when His children were sick they would come to Him in prayer. Some would be angry and not be able to hear Him. Others would use this down time to sort out their lives.

Many of Jesus' children had developed poor eating habits as a result of the fast pace they lived. Too many of His children developed compulsive behaviors as a by-product of their hectic life styles. Far too many sought the comfort of drugs and alcohol. Many had deprived their souls for so long they had no connection with the spiritual side of life and as a result, they looked to the acquisition of things to soothe their anxiety. Jesus knew material things would soon be a great cause of discomfort and sorrow for many. He knew when these things were taken away, when people could no longer find comfort in what was of the world, they would turn to Him.

Satan of course was banking on man's complacency and his lack of faith to keep him from knowing his heavenly Father, to keep him from understanding what is of God. Satan had worked so long and so hard to destroy the church. He made certain the Catholic Church would be under such attack. What better way than to promote sexual promiscuity among the clergy. Satan was most satisfied with the way things had turned out in this regard. The news media did such a great job of ensuring all in the world knew of these sexual assaults of the young. Of course, Satan made sure religion would get a bad rap in many regards. Satan could always count on the news to report the negative. Humans were not aware of how much influence Satan had on the news media. "Anything for a story" is the mind set for many in the journalism profession. Bad news travels twice as fast as good. Satan had all but destroyed the church.

Jesus knew those who truly knew Him would worship Him in the sanctity of their own homes, if need be. Soon there would come a time when a new church would be formed, one church in which all could worship. He so looked forward to when He and all of His children would reign together on earth.

Satan was working in full force now and as a result was causing much unrest. He knew who Jesus' chosen people were and Jesus knew they would all be under severe attack in the not too distant future. That is why so many had been enjoying a respite from their mission.

He knew, for example, Wendy and Jillian had often felt they had failed the Father, yet in truth, what they had experienced was merely a training time in which they would reconnect with the Father and relearn all they had once known about joy. Many of His chosen felt they had failed Him up until now. Now, they were awakening to a full understanding of the times. They were beginning to understand why they had been granted this respite. They were about to embark on the journey for which they were created.

Jesus would see to it His *earth angels* would have the strength to accomplish their mission. He knew each had been blessed with the necessary gifts and talents they would need to do His bidding. These gifts would allow them to accomplish each task which was set before them. He would see to it they would band together to form the alliance they would need to get the job done. He felt confident they had all learned not to let their egos keep them from leaning on one another. There would be no place for the ego in these times. Each and every one of His children could be confident in their gifts, understanding they had no reason to covet the gifts of one another. It would take a village to accomplish the tasks at hand. Jesus knew their ability to work together would help all to survive the storms to come. Those who were filled with the trappings of evil were the ones who were being led by Satan. No, His chosen people had learned their lessons well.

Jesus also knew since Wendy and Jillian had arrived on earth, many more *earth angels* had followed. He also knew there were some of His children who were very old souls, able to listen to what their hearts were telling them. They would present a formidable force for Satan to deal with. If man could step back a moment in time to gaze through the heavenly windows he would find much joy and so much to look forward to.

Why mankind had done his best to negate this reality was beyond the angel's comprehension. Of course, St. Michael knew this was a direct result of Satan convincing man to disregard the unseen. Man would soon learn the predicament his intellect had created. The world

Jillian 8/2012

relied on so much technology to survive. Man would be hard pressed to know how to survive when his gadgets were taken away.

The chosen ones must expose Satan's tactics. As much as faith is the belief in that which cannot be seen, evil has camouflaged itself and become woven into the very fiber of man's core existence. Man must be given the tools to defend himself from the enemy. Michael and the other angels were familiar with Satan's tactics as they watched their beloved humans fall prey to him, time and time again.

This would not be an easy task for His chosen people, the *earth angels* who now inhabited the earth. The Lord would provide them with the strength they needed, still the battle would be most difficult.

The first challenge for *earth angels* would be to help others understand they had nothing to fear but fear itself, as long as they believed in the existence of our heavenly Father. St. Michael had seen how professed non-believers would cry out their Father's name when close to death. Although fear can render one helpless, it can be the impetus which directs one to a higher power. It can open one's eyes to what is the reality and what is the illusion.

"Michael, how can we help?" The younger cherubs inquired.

"Oh, my little ones, you can help by praying for the many souls on earth who are under attack. Your prayers are so very powerful and are needed more than ever. Pray specifically now that the people on earth will come to know our heavenly Father before it is too late. Pray for the chosen ones who need as much help from the heavens as we can provide."

St. Michael was no stranger to the many effects fear could have on a human being. Therefore, he knew the first priority for *earth angels* would be to help those on earth to rise above their fears. Many had been complacent for so long they had no comprehension of what Satan had accomplished. The recent attack on America's financial structure had taken many by surprise and rendered them helpless. Humans had to be shown they were not helpless. They must understand the Lord is their shepherd who will lead them to still waters.

Humans must not allow themselves to become victims to evil. They must understand what truly matters. Satan and his evil army have no control over one's spirit because they do not know what comes from within. In other words, what Satan doesn't know, Satan, cannot attack. In truth, Satan had become quite cocky lately, which is never a good characteristic to have in battle as it makes one quite careless. This is what St. Michael and the elders were banking on. Although Satan had done quite a job, initially, of discouraging the Father's chosen ones, he had not paid much attention to them of late. What he did not know or could not know, was the Father had assured His chosen ones He would let them know when the time was right to begin their true work. Many of the chosen ones, such as Wendy and Jillian, had undergone intense training to be prepared for these times. They were well rested as Jesus had made certain they had a fair amount of respite prior to this battle.

Yes, His army was now coming together and was ready for the battle of all times! Wendy and Jillian knew they must not allow those around them to become victims to the perilous times. They must show others how to rise above their challenges. In order to survive, mankind must now listen to the Divine; the reality. Man must shed his ego and replace it with the armor of faith. He must not put his faith in worldly things. He must put His faith in what is of the Father's kingdom. In this respect, the timing could not be more perfect, for when one is on his knees he will look up. What Wendy and the others needed to do was to be where they could be heard; to make themselves available to those who were now struggling in ways they never thought possible.

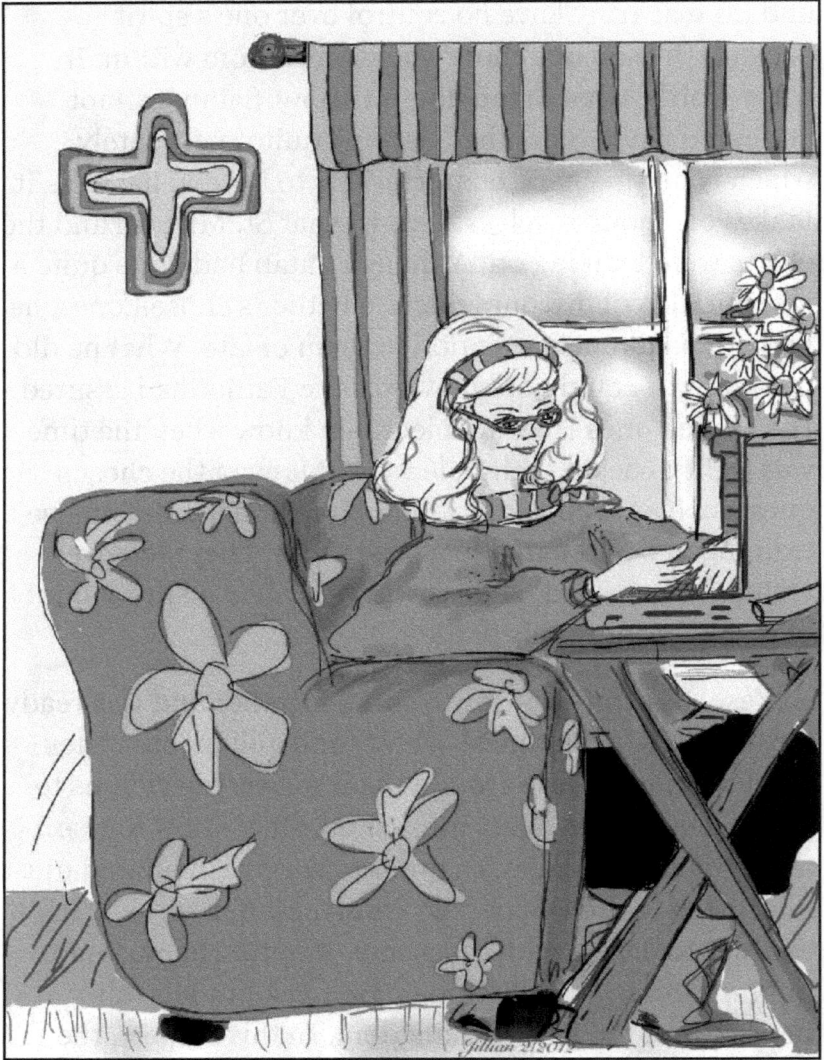

One thing for certain was *earth angels* must encourage
those they connected with to not allow themselves to
become victims. They must help them to see what truly
matters and is of lasting value. This battle could be
the catalyst to bring families closer together. These

challenges could eliminate the distractions with which Satan had so cunningly enticed them with.

Wendy, for some time had been writing daily messages she had been receiving from Jesus while in communion with him. She felt an extreme urgency to compile these messages in the book Jesus was asking her to write. She was working feverishly now. Wendy and Jillian knew if they could expose Satan for what he was many would be saved. They knew the ways of Satan and were now prepared to teach what the Father had taught them about joy. They would teach "The Art of Joy-filled Living" to those around them, enabling all to arise victorious over the evil which had inhabited their world for so long.

"We must not be afraid, Jillian!" proclaimed Wendy. "We must teach others how to go to the cave within for this is where they will get the answers they seek. We must teach them to pray as never before. We must help others to understand *religion is not the same as faith.* There are so many who need to feel our Father's comfort and strength at this time."

"Yes, I know, Wendy," Jillian replied. "I feel the urgency of the times, and I know we must do all that we can now. How do you think we should start? Do you think we should hold our joy classes again? Do you think there is time for the book to be published?"

Wendy often wondered the same things but knew in her heart she would not be led to write the book or to teach what the Father had taught her if there wasn't enough time to make a difference. She also knew the

Father never wasted anything. All that He had taught the two of them, from the beginning, would be for naught if there was not sufficient time for them to fulfill their mission.

Wendy and Jillian must let the world know in no uncertain times how very real the heavenly Father is. They must let the world know how alive He is in these times, as alive now as He was 2000 years ago!

For a long time Wendy and Jillian had avoided sharing many of their experiences with those around them. Not because they were afraid of what others would think, but because they knew the Father wanted others to come to Him because they desired to have a relationship with Him and not because they were in search of the mystical. Wendy and Jillian knew now was the time to share their experiences; to assure people how very real the heavenly Father is.

Those who knew Wendy and Jillian had often commented how much the two of them resembled one another. Wendy remembered only too well the day she and Jillian saw Jesus in the local grocery store, right around the time she and Jillian had formed ABBA and Company. She still remembered the conversation she and Jillian had regarding the name they had chosen for their company. Both knew once they named their new-found company ABBA there would be no turning back from such a commitment. Had they fully understood the magnitude of the next ten years they might have reconsidered. Yet, as *earth angels* they were predestined to fulfill their mission on earth. Even though they had no recollection of their heavenly kingdom, each knew at a very deep level they could not turn away from what they felt compelled to do.

Oh, if only Wendy and Jillian could have seen their beloved Angel of Joy as she watched them form the beginning stages of what she knew they had been created for. Those in the heavens were dancing in the streets when Jesus proclaimed the first stage of the long awaited plan had begun; a plan which some might say was the Greatest Plan on earth!

The Angel of Joy watched as she saw Jesus approach the two of them in the grocery store. Oh, if only the others could have seen the look on their faces! Joy was filled with glee knowing what was about to take place. Wendy and Jillian had stopped into the store to quickly pick up a few things for dinner. They were running late and were quite preoccupied.

Suddenly, as if out of nowhere a voice asked, *"Wendy, are the two of you sisters? You look so much alike."* They were asked this question so often at times it seemed far easier to simply say yes, which was her immediate response. Even now Wendy could remember what she felt the minute she looked up. There gazing into the very depths of her being was the most beautiful man she had ever seen. When He looked at her she knew this man was not just looking at her. He was looking into her very soul. It was at this moment Wendy knew without a shadow of a doubt she had just come face to face with her beloved Jesus; the Jesus she never doubted existed and now here He was. Oh, of all times for her to tell a white lie!

"Oh, my gosh!" exclaimed Wendy, "I am so sorry
I said we are sisters, it is just so many people ask us this
question. It is simply a lot easier for me to say yes, rather
than explain."

Jesus smiled as only He can and kindly said, *"Well, if you two are not sisters then you must have been together for a very long time!"* Wendy was afraid to look at Jillian. She was afraid to utter what she thought for fear Jillian would think her mad. Before she could even speak she knew by simply looking at Jillian that she, too, knew it was Jesus! The two were in shock.

It was not that they did not believe such an encounter was possible, the store simply was not a place one would expect to see their beloved Father. If only they would have known what the Angel of Joy knew. This moment would be embedded in their memories until the end of time.

The Angel of Joy now understood what Jesus had assured her of from the very beginning. He alone would protect Wendy and Jillian. He would make certain they had all they needed to see them through their trials. What better way than to make a visit to earth so they would be assured of His presence? His appearance would confirm their origin and would help them to know they were sent on an important mission. Little did they know how much reassurance this chance meeting would provide them in the ensuing years ahead.

Those who have seen Jesus say once you have seen Him you will never be the same. Even though one has this experience it can be difficult to believe. Wendy often thought she would have thought herself quite mad had Jillian not seen Him as well. Wendy and Jillian tried to follow Jesus, but by the time Jillian ran out to the parking lot He had disappeared.

Not until many years later did they fully understand the meaning of this meeting, and Him saying they had been together for a very long time. Now of course, as an *earth angel*, they fully understood this was the intent of this first visit; to let them know they were on a mission, a mission that had been planned in the heavens. However, not until a few months ago did they understand now was truly the time for which each had been sent.

You would not be human if you were not curious as to what Jesus looked like. As a matter of fact, Jillian and Wendy had seen Jesus on more than one occasion, but first things first. No, He wasn't in a long flowing robe. He was wearing khakis, a white T-shirt and, of course, sandals. His hair was a curly, dark sable color and flowed down to his shoulders. To say He was immaculate does not seem adequate. His eyes were a black-brown which, as said earlier, seemed to penetrate one's very being.

Once you see Jesus your life will not be the same. Your life will be forever changed. This encounter would provide them with the assurance they would need to stay the course in the years to come. This experience helped Wendy and Jillian to KNOW without a doubt they were here to do His works! It was at this point they became aware that Satan also knew they were working for our heavenly Father. They were stronger now and more aware of how the adversary operates!

Although one does not want to even acknowledge Lucifer, Wendy knew she was to share another experience. This is only being shared because you need to understand Jesus will protect you when you are under attack. You need only call His name. Where there is good, there is evil. Not fully recognizing this fact has allowed Satan to cause much destruction over time. Once Satan learned Jillian and Wendy actually formed ABBA he knew he needed to do his very best to discourage them from their task.

Not long after Jillian and Wendy saw Jesus they went to visit Father Hervy in Buckley, Washington. Father Hervy was one of the most faith filled priests they had ever met. He agreed to let them deliver a presentation on joy at the annual Woman's luncheon. Wendy was most nervous about this luncheon as she was not Catholic. Jillian came from a very strong Catholic background and her mother had arranged the invite. And so it was they agreed to meet at her mother's house. When He asked Wendy of her credentials, or why she thought she could speak about joy, the only thing she could think of to say was of course the truth, that she had always loved Jesus. Wendy was so nervous anticipating what this man would think of her. Maybe he wouldn't let her speak at the luncheon! Instead, he told her about a book called *Joshua*, written by Joseph Girzone and asked that she read it, assuring her since she loved Jesus so much she would truly love the book.

Naturally, the first thing Jillian and Wendy did was rush out and buy a copy of *Joshua*. That night while resting in bed Wendy decided to read *Joshua*. It captivated her. This was the Jesus she had always known and loved. After a short while a bright light entered the room and at this precise moment Wendy felt a dark presence as well. She felt as though a film was covering her whole being and was unable to speak. She was unable to cry out to Jillian in the other room. Wendy silently said the name of Jesus over and over again! Then the feeling passed and the room was as it had been before filled with white light. This is not brought up to scare you. It is brought up because it did happen! You must understand Jesus can protect you from attack; simply call His name and He will be there along with His guardian angels.

St. Michael and the angels of heaven have been warring against Lucifer and his fallen angels for some time. This little event caused Wendy quite a stir. It caused Wendy to revisit whether or not she really wanted to work for the Father. Naturally, she wanted to go home and think about what indeed had transpired. Yet, after a few days went by she knew she would not turn her back on her calling; the mission she had been created for.

If Wendy and Jillian had only had one such visitation, perhaps they would have felt this may have been a figment of their imagination, although they would have always wondered. But Jesus came to them on different occasions over the next few years.

It saddens one to know there are more people who have had similar experiences and for whatever reason have chosen to remain silent. We appeal to all who have had experiences with the Divine that they come forward; for it is in sharing these experiences other *earth angels* will find comfort. They can take solace in knowing others also know what they say is God's Honest Truth!

Part 3

Chapter 6

The Inauguration

Wendy could not shake the feelings of impending doom which permeated her soul. She prayed the feelings she was experiencing were not due to some hidden prejudice. This was a historic day. The first African-American had been elected President of the United States. As she sits glued to the television, there is an apprehension, a sadness she cannot articulate. She ends a phone conversation with Jillian, a conversation which leaves her even more ill at ease. There is so much to come. There is so much the average human being is not aware of at this time. There are so many hopeful people. There are so many looking to him to solve the serious economic issues which have crippled the US; a crippling which had not been experienced since the Great Depression. Wendy knew and felt it was just a matter of time before the United States fell. Why did she mark this moment, as a moment, she knew was a turning point in ways one could not even imagine? Yes, it is the first African-American President to be chosen. This showed

United States citizens are able to unite, that we are strong and wise enough to withstand the enemy.

"Yet what is the enemy? What is it mankind is not understanding at this time?" Wendy questioned, as the people and officials at the ceremony bowed their heads to say the Lord's Prayer. "As Christians we pray for your will in these times." Yet, why does she feel there are many who do not understand? Why is it there are so many who are not focusing on the heart of the matter? The heart of the matter is the evil which surrounds our new President, the evil that has been allowed to weave its ugly head into the fabric of society. It will take an army of God's chosen people to withstand what is to come. No one can possibly imagine. This is the beginning of the end of life as Americans know it today. There are so many hopeful looking to this man to make the changes needed to save our economy; to create an economy which will provide jobs and affordable health care for all and turn the tide of global warming which threatens mankind's very existence. This is such a tall order for one human being. "Man is intrinsically good," Wendy kept saying to herself, "In the end good would prevail."

Wendy knew all too well Lucifer now was at the height of his reign. He would not stop. He would do all in his power to stamp out good. Wendy knew the fallen angels were forming their legion at a very fast pace. These were the times when God's chosen were to stand up for Him. These were the times they must lead the way for others to follow. Wendy knew she must draw on the wisdom and the strength of the Lord. So much time had passed since she and Jillian formed ABBA and Company; so much time had passed since their initial face-to-face encounter with Jesus. She prayed with every ounce of her being the Lord would show her each day what she was called to do. She prayed for the wisdom to know and hear what was of Him.

Wendy was wise to the wiles of Satan and knew she and the others would be under direct attack now. She knew many in the country were feeling the same thing at the same time. This was not a time for the faint of heart. This was a time for all who knew the Lord to be still and listen to what He was saying. In going to the cave within each of his children will understand their true calling.

It is a time now to not be swayed by the external. It is a time to listen to the still voice within. Wendy knew she was called to show others the importance of going to the cave within, for in the end this safe haven will be one's saving grace. It is difficult to hear this voice as there are so many external distractions in the world at this time.

Satan uses materialism to distract humans from seeing what they need to see and also causes them to accept a form of government which will open the door for Satan to enter each and every home. Mankind will no longer have the freedom of democracy. Mankind will readily relinquish control of his own surroundings. Although subtle in the beginning, by the time one understands what has come, it will be too late. This is what Satan will want one to think. Wendy knew if man could but listen, to what comes from the center of their being, good would triumph.

As she listens to Obama speak she hears him say, "We must begin the work of rebuilding America." She wonders at what cost this rebuilding will be done. Mankind's complacency will surely be his demise. Many need to listen now. Many need to believe. Wendy knew the change must come from within. The strength and wisdom must come from within. She knew many once again were looking to the externals. Many were willing to blame others for the state of the nation. Wendy recalls the fall of the Roman Empire. Is America to experience the same outcome? Does the heart of America exemplify the values of a Christian? Do the citizens of America know Jesus? Do they have a relationship with Him? This in the end will be all that matters.

Obama talks about the enemy advancing in the winter of our hardship. "When we were tested we refused to let this journey end. America will overcome in the face of adversity." Wendy heard these valiant words. Wendy knew all too well the tools of the enemy. She also knew Satan would pull out his full arsenal now. Most did not understand. Most did not recognize his tools. He had so many tools she could understand why one wasn't able to easily recognize what had become part of their everyday life. Mankind's ego Wendy knew, for the most part, ruled the hearts of America. People of power and position no longer heard the voice of our heavenly Father. Pumped up with self importance and self edification, corruption had permeated the financial foundation of America. These tentacles would eventually reach into every home in the heartland. These were Wendy's thoughts during this most momentous event.

Wendy knew many hopeful hearts were looking to this new leader for wisdom. They were looking to him for a solution in these desperate times, which she knew were certain to worsen. She knew with every ounce of her being this was just the beginning. She prayed for the President, yet she feared if Americans did not wake up this was the beginning of the end.

"How could one be joyous? How could one look forward to what was to come? The new President speaks of a collective failure on the part of the people of the United States," Wendy questioned. She knew this only proved what progress Satan had made to date. All were responsible for the state of the nation. The nation was in financial distress. Wendy knew all too well what was at the core of this distress. The moral fiber of America had deteriorated to such a level it was difficult for the average being to fully comprehend. This moral decay was largely due to one of Satan's strongest tools; the tool of complacency. Even though most were aware of what did not align with their moral fiber, often they would look the other way, saying to themselves they were not responsible and not able to make a difference. It was this very attitude and thought process that paved the way for Lucifer!

It was man's self serving attitude which caused him to close his heart to what his soul was crying out for; to what was at the center of his being. Man's soul was in anguish not understanding the importance of following the Lord's commandments which had been set since the beginning of time. Why did mankind refuse to follow the commandments? Wendy knew man's free will allowed him to mold and reshape these commandments in order to justify and satisfy the longings of the ego. The standards of the ego now controlled many parts of the world and most certainly the United States. Wendy was being called upon to teach all she and Jillian had been taught. She must listen with all her heart and put other interests aside.

The angels in heaven were on full alert as they knew what was to come in a very short time. Americans were to be challenged as never before. That which they had built their security on was now to be toppled. Man was not prepared for what was to come. How could mankind fight if he did not hear what his soul was crying out for? The world they knew today, the security which they had built around them, was being severely challenged.

Most humans did not understand the full measure of evil which was running rampant in the world. Most did not know how to defend themselves from such an evil. The angels knew there were many *earth angels* who needed their assistance more than ever before. It made them weep to think of the suffering that was to come as a result of man's complacency; complacency which was manifested by Satan. There were so many distractions in the everyday life of an American. These distractions were part and parcel of materialism, driving people to acquire what they coveted. Many times consumerism was at the core of their very ideals.

These distractions did not allow time for prayer but occupied their minds to such a degree there was no time to nurture their souls. Jesus would use this time to awaken as many souls as possible. The Lord loves His children with all His heart, yet many would not hear; many would not be listening. Mankind's response to these times could destroy the world they knew.

So many were now looking to the government for answers. Yet, Wendy, the heavenly angels, and Jesus knew the heart of the government needed to change. The hearts of individuals in power needed to change. Self-serving interests must be put aside. Jesus knew Satan's tentacles were wrapped around the very core of America.

St. Michael watched as Wendy began to understand the nature of the times. He remembered all too well the conversation Jesus held with Wendy many years ago. Jesus had told Wendy when the time was right she would know; she would remember all. He could see what Jesus foresaw was now happening. Wendy was remembering. At last Wendy fully understood her purpose and her origin. She would not be deterred or distracted. Her guardians would look over her as never before and all obstacles would be removed. There was no time for delay. Satan must be put in his place. He must be thwarted. Wendy would teach. She would write to open the eyes of others so they might see the wiles of Satan. They would understand the tools of the adversary and come to understand and to recognize the voice within. In this understanding they would come to know the true meaning of life. They would come to know where their true security comes from. Their eyes would be cast now on what was of the spirit, not what was of the ego. They would realize it is in knowing their true purpose one can make a difference in the world. Wendy knew there were enough gifts to go around. Humans must now use their God-given gifts fully, understanding man's responsibility to his fellow man.

There was so much work to be done, so much to be defined, yet Wendy knew she and Jillian were not alone in this battle. The time was prime. The time was now! The art of joy-filled living was needed more than ever. It would be taught and the world would listen, for it is in the times of sorrow one can find joy. Many must be on their knees before they can look up. This time is an opportunity for change and for the Lord's light to shine on the world. It is still up to man to alter this course. It cannot be done if there are deaf ears. One must listen as never before. St. Michael knew all of these and many more thoughts were on Wendy's heart and soul. It was up to her and Jillian to complete their mission.

Wendy and Jillian were more enthusiastic than ever. They knew in no uncertain terms these were the times they were destined for. This was what they had been waiting for since they met on earth and formed ABBA and Company.

Jesus had promised the Angel of Joy He would see to it that Wendy and Jillian would remember their heavenly origin. There were many *earth angels* on the earth now, yet Wendy and Jillian were to work together side by side to accomplish their mission. They were good students and as a result were very enthusiastic teachers when it came to the subject of joy.

You must understand during these years many were wrapped in worlds filled with material conquests and

aspirations. Religion was not practiced by the vast majority of people and many confused religion with faith, and
as a result not many individuals were interested in the
subject of joy. They felt joy was a word primarily used in
a religious setting. Even though Wendy and Jillian had
tried hard over the ensuing years, it just never seemed
to really take hold. Towards the end of 10 years it had
become such a difficult struggle, and as a result they were
slowly losing their initial enthusiasm for their mission
and wondered, why, if this was the will of their Father,
things had never evolved?

Wendy could remember the very day, the very
moment, Jesus, released the two of them from ABBA. She
could feel it at the deepest level of her soul and understood He was saying enough was enough. It was not that
He was disappointed in them it was simply He felt they
were now prepared for what was to come. Yes, now would
be time for them to enjoy a brief respite before they were
to start on their true mission.

These were now the thoughts which were going
through Wendy's mind as she, for over a month now, had
been diligently writing daily messages from Jesus. Many
times over the past few years she had tried to finish the
book "Earth Angels" but she would only write a few pages
then would stop. Now, it seemed as though the book was
quickly coming together. Jesus had assured Wendy the
words she would now write would be in the will of her
heavenly Father.

Neither, Jillian or Wendy would do anything to disappoint the Father. There were so many things happening

in the world it was difficult to focus on just one event. There was so much dis-ease manifesting in many souls. It would have been difficult to know where and how to start if it had not been for their strong communion with Jesus. Now, it was as if a light bulb had gone off in their heads. Wendy understood why she was unable to finish the book until now. These were the times they were destined for!

Wendy knew she and Jillian had not failed their precious Jesus, previously. Now was the time they were to teach. Now, was the time they were to write the book; to reassure other *earth angels* these were the times they were sent here for as well. Many would understand they must pay attention to their mission. Wendy prayed that she had written the book exactly as Jesus wanted.

There were so many signs which were being given throughout the world. These signs would serve as a warning for those who did not embrace what was of God. Satan could no longer count on the tool of complacency that had served him so well in the past. Now he would pull out his strongest weapons, fear and deception. He would see to it there would be such utter chaos throughout the world that fear would run rampant, causing many to become immobile and useless. Yes, and if fear and deception were not enough he had many other tricks up his sleeve. Little did Satan realize there were many *earth angels* who were starting to awaken, as if from a deep sleep. They had been well trained for what lie ahead. Additionally, they would go to the cave within to commune with their father. Yes, this was the secret rendezvous place for all of Jesus' little soldiers; one that would provide them with much comfort, solace and instruction over the weeks, days and months to come!

Jesus was asking Wendy and Jillian to inform others, without a shadow of a doubt, He was there waiting to hear from each of them. He had formed a covenant with His chosen prior to their assignment on earth, and would do all He could to help them succeed.

He would see to it they had one another to turn to and they would recognize one another by the fruits of their labor. There would be nothing left to chance. His *earth angels* had been equipped with all the tools they would need to succeed.

Wendy could not tell you the precise moment she understood these were the times she had been sent here for. Yet, she thoroughly understood the importance of the cave within. This is a subject Jesus had been talking to her about for many years. She wanted everyone to understand how to commune with the Father. She realized while many did commune with the Father there were many who doubted what they heard from Him in the night. Many still needed reassurance they were on track and they had not allowed the imaginings of their mind to obscure what was of Jesus. She knew it would take much discipline to stay on track and not allow the signs of the time to distract or negate them from their calling.

There were so many disasters happening in the world it was difficult for Wendy and Jillian to stay focused on one particular event. Although situations were different, it was easy to see the tangled web of evil Satan had created. Many displayed a lack of belief in God. He was no longer mentioned in the public arena and many of the younger generations had not been taught the basics of religion and certainly did not understand the measure of faith. Countries were now at war within themselves and many at war with each other. The period of unrest was now increasing at such a rapid rate it was difficult to stay abreast of current events. There were many significant natural disasters occurring in such a short span of time. One could hardly keep on top of the demands that needed to be met. As a result of these natural disasters, food prices were rising and there now appeared to be a major shortage in gasoline.

Yes, the pot was certainly getting stirred up and it only looked as though things were to get worse. Even now as Wendy was writing, Japan had just experienced a major earthquake resulting in the worst tsunami of all time. The media had captured much of the horrific details. It was a perfect time for Satan to unleash major doses of fear. As if that weren't enough, the nuclear facilities were now unprotected, and damaged so much there was a great deal of anticipation regarding the onslaught of radiation throughout the universe.

As Satan was standing back rubbing his sweaty palms, he did not realize there was a legion of *earth angels* who would be joining hands together on earth. Yes, He had gravely underestimated those who were part and parcel of the Divine. So, even though it seemed to many these were the darkest of days, Satan was in for the fight of his life. He and his army were about to come against a most formidable force, for Jesus and the Arch Angels had planned their strategy well. They would use these events for the betterment of mankind. They would use these myriad of events as a wakeup call for many. It is through these events there would be many souls who would come to know and understand the truth. They would come to know Jesus.

Many years ago Satan exclaimed "In the end your people will turn on you, they will deny knowing you, of this you can be certain! " Jesus knew without a shadow of a doubt nothing could be farther from the truth for He would see to it every detail would be attended to. Yes, this was truly the **Greatest Plan** Jesus had ever devised and He knew it would not fail!

Wendy knew there would be much in store for many in the days ahead. She knew that now was the time for all to spend as much time in communion with their Father as possible. It is in this communion they will find the answers and the reassurance they are seeking. Jesus had told Wendy a long time ago she was a writer. He had told her a long time ago she would be writing about the Greatest Plan on earth and now twenty years later she finally knew, for certain, what that plan was. She and many others would be part of this Great Plan and would play an active role in bringing about His kingdom on earth.

Wendy and Jillian were certain there would be many who understood the importance of sharing their gifts willingly with one another, for now they would see it is in the coming together of these gifts great works will be accomplished. These are the ones who will initiate a new way of life for all. They will set an example for many to follow and the current standards man has set will no longer prevail, for this kingdom will not be ruled by that which is of the ego. It will be ruled by what is of the Divine nature. It will be ruled by what is the higher nature. **Right and mindful decisions will be made!** They will be decisions that are in the best interest of all, not for the interest of a select few. It will be a kingdom ruled by the Divine and as a result agape love will flourish. Peace and harmony will prevail and there will be no disease as known by man today. One must remember then through sorrow comes joy. One must look to the light in the days and weeks ahead knowing God will indeed provide the way and we, his willing soldiers, will respond to His call. It has already been written and so it shall be. His kingdom shall indeed reign on this earth!

The Angels in heaven were singing as they could see Wendy, Jillian and many others were listening to what the Divine was saying. There were so many now who were paying close attention to the signs that were being given. Although it was difficult to watch many of the events unfold, the angels had been prepared in advance for what would occur now on earth. These events had been a long time in coming, even in angelic measurements of time. It was hard to see the suffering as they knew there would be more to come, but this time the suffering would result in joy as goodness would prevail, and in the end evil would exist, no more.

The Angel of Joy had to smile as she remembered Wendy's distaste for mankind's free will, yet in truth free will had allowed man to choose what in the end would cause the destruction of many. The angels knew there would come a time when evil would be destroyed. This is what all angelic beings were focused on. There were many battles being fought in the heavens now, as they were being fought on earth, for this was the final battle between good and evil as it exists throughout the universe.

Every time a rainbow occurs Joy knew there would be many who would be reminded of the covenant Jesus has formed with His chosen people. The Angel of Joy was smiling as she saw the joy on Jillian's face, on one particular afternoon while she was out fishing, as she noticed a rainbow overhead. It was Joy's idea to have Jillian take a picture of this rainbow and send it to Wendy on her cell phone just as she was writing this page in the book. This is an example of the little promptings angels are sending His people at this time.

One can be assured that as an *earth angel* you are being guided now by your heavenly counterparts. They are by your side day and night and will be with you as you establish His kingdom on earth. Pay attention then to the little things as that is their way of reassuring you of their presence, in these times.

Chapter 7

In The Heavens

You will also see many miracles as in the days of old. This is the way Jesus will awaken many souls in these times. You must ask to see the world through the eyes of the Divine and listen to what the spirit is calling you to do. For all, Divine guidance is being given at this time. One must wonder why it has taken Wendy and Jillian so long to act on accomplishing their mission. First, you must understand the human conditions they are faced with on a daily basis, as are the rest of God's chosen people. Even *earth angels* are subject to a myriad of distractions. You must also remember they are free to choose on a daily basis what they want to do.

Secondly, you must remember this is a war against good and evil, so it should not be a big surprise, to those in the heavens, and on earth. Satan, is using every tool he can to deter Wendy and Jillian from their mission. Although he could not know the magnitude of their assignment, or the details involved, Satan has known the important job Wendy and Jillian would have in the final battle.

Many in the heavenly realm were anxious now. If the truth be known there were many who felt Wendy just wasn't getting it. Often they would see her sit down to write only to set it aside time and time again; only to turn a deaf ear to what they felt she should be hearing in the night. Jesus knew it was not that Wendy and Jillian were not listening, for He knew each was trying to listen in their own way, but He knew they were subject to a myriad of distractions. Jesus knew they would succeed because of their faithfulness and intense love of Him. He felt confident they would be the strong soldiers they had been prepared to be. Satan and his army knew Wendy and Jillian had suffered much discouragement over the years and was unleashing all his tools to keep them distracted.

Now they were getting it! They were becoming more implanted in their Father's kingdom. They knew without a shadow of a doubt what they were called to do. The Angel of Joy was so elated, as she could see how fast and furiously Wendy was now writing. Joy had to admit there was a moment when she thought Jillian and Wendy were falling away from each other. There was a brief period of turmoil in their relationship and each had come dangerously close to going their separate ways (or so each other thought). Jesus knew that would never happen. He knew the love they held for each other. He had faith the two of them would understand they had been together throughout eternity. Satan had certainly tried his best to tear them apart. Jesus knew of Satan's plans to cast doubt on their mission. That is why Jesus was keeping a close watch on them. He had promised them He would give them what they needed to complete their assignment.

The time was getting dangerously close when there would be much calamity on earth. Satan was setting in motion events that would set mankind on his heels and open the door for evil to strike. He would use the strongest and most effective tools in his arsenal. There were many *earth angels* at this time who knew their calling, yet many needed guidance and reassurance in the final days ahead.

"Father how much more is Wendy to write?" asked Joy. "I know she is trying so hard to respond to what You are saying, yet I cannot help but feel this book must be given top priority! Why, just look at the way Satan is attacking our chosen people. They are all lifting up so many prayers now and I am afraid they do not understand how this will all come together, as we in the heavens understand it to be. Why can they not see that this is the beginning of your Great Plan Father?"

"Oh my dear Joy, while you are most anxious you above all, must understand timing now is of the utmost importance," Jesus answered. *"We cannot allow Satan to get the upper hand. I know it seems as though there has been a great deal of delay. Yet, you must trust if I had wanted this to be available sooner I would have made certain such is the case. You must rejoice now My little one. For you and the others are about to see the fruits of their labor come into fruition. You are about to see the*

*beginning of My master plan come into being. Once the
book is written there will be others who will assist them
in the publication and from then on things will advance
at a very fast pace."*

The Angel of Joy was listening intently now to every
word Jesus spoke. She knew she had trained Wendy and
Jillian well. She also knew the attack they would be under
once the book was published. She knew St. Michael had
been on high alert for some time now. She only hoped
that he would personally watch over the two of them.

St. Michael and his legion were on high alert as the
battles were increasing in the heavenly realms on a daily
basis now, not to mention the uprisings which were
occurring on a daily basis, in the Middle East. Why these
activities alone were keeping St. Michael very busy to say
the least. The Angel of Joy was well aware of how very
busy St. Michael was at this time. She prayed he would be
giving his utmost attention to Wendy and Jillian.

St. Michael was well aware of the concerns the Angel of
Joy had regarding Wendy and Jillian. He would do everything in his power to see to it they succeeded. No, The Angel
of Joy need not worry in his regard. After all he loved each
of them just as much as Joy did and would do everything he
could to assist them in the days and weeks to come.

Jesus could see the Angel of Joy was most anxious for
Wendy and Jillian. He had been communing with Wendy
on a daily basis and knew she was writing what He had
told her in their conversations. He would make certain
she would share her writings with Jillian on a daily basis

also, as this would save time when the book was ready
to be compiled. He also knew even though Wendy was
writing, she needed to have time to fully understand what
He had told her. He was not concerned she would write
what was not of Him, as she had been very cautious in
this regard. Jesus knew how He wanted the book to be
formatted and for this reason was showing her bits and
pieces of what she had already written in the past. He had
planned it this way, as He wanted all the pieces to come
together with ease for her and Jillian.

Wendy loved the time she spent in conversation with
Jesus. She knew He was giving her the words to write
and looked forward with anticipation to the book being
completed. She knew without a shadow of a doubt Jesus
would let her know when the time had come.

"Jesus, how will she know when the time is right to
compile the book?" questioned Joy. Are there still more
events which need to transpire before this can happen? "

*"There will be many events to come. Wendy and
Jillian understand the urgency of completing the book in
preparation for that time."* explained Jesus

"Should she change how it is written Father? I have
seen her write daily messages from you now. Do you
think those on earth will finally believe these writings are
of the Divine?" Perhaps it would be best if they wrote all
in a fictional sense?"

"Oh my dear Joy, why do you concern yourself so?"
Jesus chuckled. *"You must have faith in this matter*

knowing those who know will indeed believe these writings are of the Divine. They need only write that which they know to be the truth. They only need to write that which they have been guided to write and all will be well. For I tell you if I did not want the writings in this manner it would have already been written so. **Others must know when they go to the cave within they indeed are capable of hearing that which if of Me. They will know that which is of Me and that which is not. When they go to this sanctuary they will find the safe harbor they all are seeking in these times. Therefore, this book will show all what they can glean from listening to Me. This book will show them that which I want my chosen to understand in these times. This book will indeed be a tool for my earth angels to wage war against the adversary. It will give one then that which they need to know in order to proceed with that which they are called to do. It will assist them in their higher purpose and provide them the confidence they need to proceed**. There are so many of My children now who need the comfort of knowing there are many like them on this earth in these final days. This book should provide them with this comfort. This book will then help arm them for battle.

I want My children to understand the importance of the words which are written. I want them to open their hearts. I want all of My children now to spend more time in communion with Me. This book, **My book**, will show My children how to actively commune with Me. I will bring those people to My children, as needed, to assist each one of them in that which they are called to do.

Those who know Wendy will understand the nature of the book, and still there will be some who do not know who will come to understand through that which is written in these pages. There will be something there for everyone who reads the book. I have left nothing to chance and I have left no one out. If there is a message which needs to be written it will be found in these pages. If there is an answer you are seeking you will find the answer in these pages. There is something for everyone, of that you can be certain. For if you have come to read this book then it was sent to you by the Divine.

I have formed a covenant with My children. They must all believe now they are being guided. They must understand that which is their higher purpose and plant their feet firmly on the ground. They already are aware of the tools Satan has been using. Yet, they must be on high alert now for that which is to come. They all need to live in the moment and pay attention to the signs I am sending at this time. For I and My legion now can leave nothing to chance. All must reflect on the Lord's Prayer. **Thy kingdom come Thy will be done!**

My chosen people shall help bring My kingdom to earth. They will accomplish this with a higher understanding, with a wisdom that has been foretold since the beginning of time! All of My children are being alerted now. Satan shall not win for the covenant I have formed with My children cannot and will not be broken!"

The Angel of Joy so enjoyed listening to Jesus' enthusiastic proclamations! It also caused her wings to flutter with anticipation! She knew it was just a matter of time before she would be reunited with her beloved protégés! She knew they could feel her presence now more than ever. She could hardly wait to embrace each in her angelic arms. Yes, there were exciting days ahead! When all was accomplished there would be much rejoicing in the heavens. **When the angels all sing one will know the Great Plan has finally come into fruition.** It is when the angels sing, all, once again, shall be reunited on earth. Hallelujah! For all will have completed what they have been sent to do!

Part 4

Chapter 8

Earth Angels Guidebook

Wendy's Journal of Daily Conversations with Jesus

Wendy felt an increasing desire to write as never before. The Lord had told her to write on a daily basis now. He assured her these writings were indeed meant to be shared with other "Earth Angels" in these times.

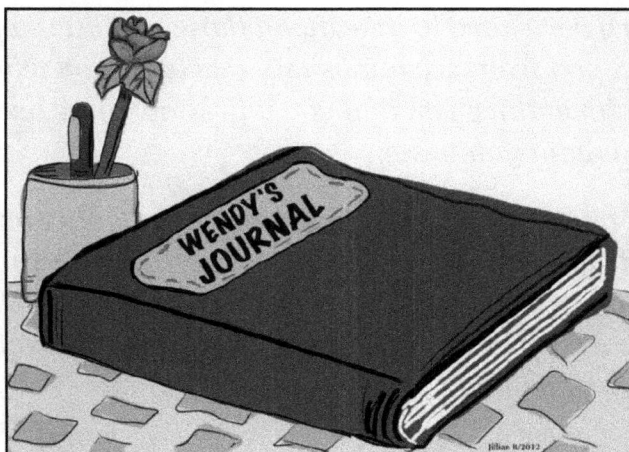

"In an effort not to change or alter the material received while in communion with our Father we have left all writings in their original text. The writings which have been included, although at times personal, apply to all his children. It is our fervent prayer the following pages will be a source of renewal and enlightenment for all." **Wendy and Jillian**

2/12/2011

What is an *earth angel*? *A messenger who inhabits the earth and works for God.*

"It is time now to just listen and write that which comes to your mind My little one, it will be far easier this way and then we can edit that which I do not want in the journal. What I told you last night must be elaborated on in the journal. For although this is simplistic in nature there are points which need to be made under each category. Be not anxious that I speak to you in the evening as you will remember that which I say and will write that which is relevant to the task at hand. You must try very hard to take away those activities which distract you from accomplishing this task. You will be filled with enthusiasm and you will know these are the words I want you to say.

*You must point out to My children I will always validate to them that which is the truth. **When I want to make myself known it will come to you three fold**. Each earth angel will receive confirmation of that which I am calling them to do in this manner. You then*

*need not worry that I have not made clear My will
for you.*

*You cannot force things in your time and must trust
all works together in My time to bring about that which
you need to complete your mission. I will send the tools
to you that you need at precisely the right time of this
you can be certain.*

*There are many in My heavenly kingdom watching
out for My chosen at this time and will assist you in their
prayerful manner to insure you are paying attention to
the signs at hand.*

*Now as earth angels I do not want you to dwell
on that which you cannot control. This in itself is a
distraction and will keep each of you from fulfilling
and understanding your own purpose.*

*You have been given free will so that you can fully
understand the challenges humans face on a daily basis.
You are not imagining that which you are. However,
I see your need for reassurance. These messages shall
provide reassurance for many or perhaps we should call
it an Earth Angel's handbook. We shall see.*

*When you desire to spend more time in prayer it is
imperative you listen to that which I am telling each of
you. Many of My earth angels are called upon in the still
of the night as that is the only time I am able to get their
complete attention. It truthfully is the one time they are
not distracted by the wiles of Satan. **For this reason
all earth angels should keep a pen and pencil by***

their bed to record that which they hear. *What one then hears in the still of the night will give light to the day (I caution do not change My words).*

I know of your struggles, all of your struggles and will send those to you who will help you in your endeavors. Pay attention to all that is around you. My earth angels should familiarize themselves with the principles of Buddha as there is much knowledge one can glean from doing so. It helps to prepare one for the true battle. You would not have an interest if there was nothing to be learned from doing so. ***Earth angels must not close their minds to learning and should not be threatened by other cultures or religions.*** *You cannot combat that which you do not understand. When you are one with the Divine you understand the need to embrace one another in the quest for spiritual enlightenment.* ***Although each journey may be very different the destination for an earth angel is always the same. Therefore, look to the destination to discover the intention of those who cross your path.***

The measure of My compassion has no limit. For I understand the challenges of free will. This free will for My earth angels was the subject of much debate in the heavenly realm. It is indeed most difficult to circumvent the wiles of Satan when free will is abound.

I love all of My children and am most concerned with their souls. It is not for you to judge. It is however for you to listen to that which I am calling you to do. I have sent many earth angels out two by two as in the days of old. Others I have sent for one specific task and so it is not necessary to have a life companion(eternal life). Just know if you are two by two there is a reason for this and you must know what our Father has put together will not be torn apart. For it will not be allowed. There may be periods of times when there is a distance between you. The same as when some of you were guardians of humans. You will always be connected in thought and spirit. It is the same for those who have been given the same mission. Do not abuse this knowledge thinking I will always intervene yet know I understand the difficulty of your mission and the importance of completing this assignment together. **Earth angels must spend time in communion with Me so they will hear that which they need to know to complete their mission in these times.** Do not, as an earth angel, seek answers from those who do not and cannot understand that which you know to be true. Simply shake the dust from your feet and carry on. **When you feel threatened ask our heavenly Father to surround you with the white light of purity. This will allow you to manifest that which is of Me in a manner which will be received. As an earth angel you are seed planters and travel where those of the clergy often can't and will not go.**

You will know when you are on track as you will be filled with enthusiasm for the task. All who know Me must understand holy enthusiasm. For that which I want accomplished comes through me. Earth angels are merely the vessel. I am the conduit and can accomplish great works through My earth angels. **When you**

are feeling less than enthusiastic your own free will has taken charge. *When you sense then lack of enthusiasm you must pray the prayer of the Divine:*

Father please clear my eyes so that I might see this situation and others through the eyes of Jesus. Open my ears so I will hear that which You would have me hear. May I speak only those words You would have me say. I pray then for a triple annointing of the Holy Spirit and that our hearts will be united as one.

Each specific earth angel has come equipped with specific gifts and talents. Therefore, it is wrong to covet the gifts of another. Although it is right to learn from one another earth angels must not spend time on that which they know is not their job. They must cultivate that which they have been given in order to accomplish their mission. It takes many hands to accomplish these heavenly tasks. **When one perfects the tools they have been given they then do not minimize the gifts of another**. *For they are at peace knowing they are doing that which they have been called upon to do. Often My works are detained because duties become confused. This is most important to understand.*

In the book Joshua, I often used carvings as My means of expression, My way of making a point so to speak. Each earth angel has a specific gift they can use in this manner. I see you are limiting My thoughts here. Let us name some gifts so that you may understand the expansiveness of these gifts. There are of course the obvious, as you My little one are writing and this is My desire for you. You think of a painter. There are so many ways and means to express oneself. It is but the conduit for that which comes from the heart. There is for example the heart surgeon who is gifted with his hands yet understands where this gift comes from and he is only the conduit. He recognizes miracles and gives credit to the Divine. There are those who have a love for the elderly, for the little children and as a result are filled with joy serving in their presence.

Earth angels must fully understand there is no such thing as coincidence in My regard. Therefore it is important they pay attention to all that is around them. Otherwise they may miss some important details or tools which will assist them in their mission.

When it seems as though there is no movement, that nothing is happening this is when the most is happening. It is the calm before the storm as there is much which is being put in place.

Earth angels become most frustrated with this as they want so much to do that which they have been sent to accomplish. You must always remember My heavenly timing is not the same as yours. **What can seem like months and years to you is only a brief second in the heavenly realm.** This is not for you to fully comprehend as you can only relate to earthly time, yet it is far different from that in the Father's kingdom. Eternity has an entirely different measurement of time than anyone on earth can understand. Even though

*you work for Me, you are, I am afraid only equipped
with limited knowledge of our Father's kingdom. This is
indeed intentional as the longing to return from whence
you came would indeed become too great and would
interfere with the work at hand.*

*An earth angel must be allowed to experience
that which appears to be negative in their regard.
For without this experience they would not have full
understanding of the frailties humans contend with.
The ethereal realm has also had a most difficult time
watching as their chosen suffer through these experiences.* **Yet, even though they are allowed I have
formed a covenant with My chosen and will not
leave them in their time of need.** *I am always there
watching, waiting, listening and yes orchestrating
what is to come next.*

*There will be those who will wonder at your bold-
ness claiming to be a messenger of the heavenly Father.
No less at your boldness in calling yourselves earth
angels. Yet, this is what you are and it is time the world
understands what is the reality and what is the illusion.*

*There are those souls who do not yet understand. As
earth angels you must share all that you have learned.*
**Every time you connect with another human
being you have a responsibility to share that
which you know to be true.** *You will be sent those
people whom I have put in your path to witness to. You
must never forget your mission and use all connections
as an opportunity to serve the heavenly Father."*

2/14/2011

"Do not doubt that which comes then from the interior. Do not doubt that which come from the center of one's being. For this is of Me. My earth angels all know the difference yet sometimes they do not respond to My call. It takes discipline and it takes practice. You must not confuse then that which is the reality and that which is the illusion.

I speak to this next part as it is very important and I want this to be in the book of that you can be certain. My children must know that which is of Me and that which is not of Me. Yet, you must be able to listen to that which I am saying. Some call it intuition, yet earth angels know that which I am calling them to do. My tasks are not measured by man's standards. You will be drawn to your purpose.

You think of magnet. Yes, that could be described as such, yet it would be better to say led by the Holy Spirit. You must remember also there are a whole host of angelic beings at this time watching over you, nudging you in the right direction.

Whenever you feel the farthest away from Me and your purpose such is not the case. For there are many things going on at once which are leading you to your purpose. *Not all of course is in your time nor can you understand the intricacies involved. When you are in My kingdom this all will*

become crystal clear but for now you must understand
this is the way of the Divine. So fear not! There will
come a time when all shall see the truth, that which
is the heart of the matter. I am speaking in terms of
mankind.

In the past I have referred to the cave within. This is
where My chosen will find solace and comfort. When
you come to Me I will give you the answers you need.
When you hear nothing then you must wait until the
answer is clear. If I want something to happen, the door
will open. If it will not serve your purpose then I will
close the door. I will open the correct door in time.
Timing, Timing, Timing! **It is heavenly time not
mans**. Take comfort in knowing this. Man's time is but
a speck in eternity.

**Wendy you are a humble person that is for
certain, yet you must not be humble in My
regard. My earth angels must accept the gifts
they have been given are for the betterment of
mankind and when used in this vain one must
have confidence and enthusiasm for the task at
hand. One can afford to be enthusiastic as it is
coming from Me!**

**Nothing in God's kingdom is ever wasted
Wendy and when you work for Me, all of your
journey is put towards the ultimate goal,
towards your life purpose, your mission. This
is important and should be included under the
three statements.**

These three statements are very important and should be emphasized in the book:

1. ***"The freedom to choose"*** *allows one to formulate their own lesson plan. Therefore, there is no such thing as a mistake. For it is in the knowing we understand this is the journey. Mistakes as mankind calls them are the catalyst for learning. This then is the pathway to wisdom. Earth angels know they have a responsibility to share this wisdom with others. This wisdom does not come easily.*

2. ***Make right and mindful decisions.*** *One has the power within themselves to achieve their hearts desire. It is only through Me they are able to make right and mindful decisions. Each then is given the appropriate tools needed to accomplish their hearts desire which is their angelic purpose, their true purpose.*

3. *Thirdly, and in this order an earth angel must then* ***exercise the power of no!*** *For it is in the knowing one then can focus on their hearts desire (Divine purpose with renewed enthusiasm).*

Much then which is being written can be included under these statements. I will show you how in the future.

Earth angels come in all different shapes and sizes. Do not disregard those you meet. ***Live each day in the moment as I need you to be aware of those who***

are around you. *This way you will not waste precious time. The time you humans are most concerned about. Many times I send messages and answers you are not paying attention to. If My people would slow down and take time to smell the roses, they would know that which they need to know. All I ask is that each day you take time to reflect on Me.*

My earth angels must understand how important communing with Me is. *They must take time to truly listen. Many times you do not hear that which I am saying. This can only be fine tuned by practice and spending time with Me.*

There will come a time when the way to Me is through this communion. It will be interior and you must be able to discern that which you hear in the still of the night. You must know when to act and when not to act. You must know when to move and when not to. This is so important for all of you at this time. It must be as though I am standing in front of you. When I look into your eyes I can reach deep into the depths of your being. This is where I am at all times, in the depths of your being. If you do not allow yourself to become unduly distracted you will know the difference. You will be more readily able to discern that which is of Me and that which is of the mind, the ego. Now I tell you this when you want confirmation of that which you hear in the night do not go to those who do not understand from whence you come. Do not open the doors for the adversary to come in. Many of you will be tempted to do so as you have those in your life who do not know Me the same as you.

This is intended. This is how you witness and also this is how you learn. If this were not the case My kingdom would already reign on this earth.

I have formed a covenant with My chosen and will never leave them. I am there for you day and night, night and day. You need only call on Me and I will be there.

When you are at a loss as to where you are in your journey, ask yourself who you work for? Ask yourself what truly matters to each of you? Earth angels know who they work for and what truly matters. Because of free will they are subject to discouragement. Because they are earth angels they are subject to attack from the adversary.

This Earth Angel guide book will give My earth angels the spiritual injection they need to jumpstart their ministry, their mission.

They must not measure their success by the standards of the ego. They know that which they have been called to do for it has never left them. I have never left them!

They have all been given a brief respite to formulate and reformulate their mission and to refine their gifts to suit the needs and the purpose of the Divine! They must use their gifts and talents now for My purposes, for the betterment of mankind.

Earth angels must learn to live in the moment! Pay attention! When I was a child I thought like a child. When I was a man I thought as a man. As an earth angel

you must have the faith of a child, yet the wisdom of My life lessons to use as a catalyst, a platform to accomplish that which is My earthly mission.

You are a writer. Write for Me! If you are a gardener, garden for Me, a painter, paint for Me; a nurse, a baker, a candlestick maker do it all for Me!

2-15-11

"You are listening now My little one and there is much to share this morning. Be not anxious as to what you are going to write. I will show you what and how to accomplish this task.

My chosen people must understand they are never alone. *Earth angels while on assignment have* heavenly angels who are specifically assigned to watch over them. I have formed a covenant with thee and this is a covenant that cannot be broken.

I want to talk to each of you about your purpose on earth. First and foremost you need not look too far for your specific purpose as **your purpose will find you.** Remember when I talked to you about **holy enthusiasm?** That which you are the most enthusiastic about, that which you never lose enthusiasm for is your purpose. Years ago I taught you that **action was passion in progress**. You act on that which you are the most passionate about. **Do not take your gifts for granted for that is a sure way to deter you from that which you have been called to do.**

Remember when I talked about coveting one another's gifts? While it is a blessed thing to admire the talents of others, an earth angel must fine tune and use the gifts I have bestowed upon them. When these gifts are shared with each other great works can be accomplished. **For no man, no angel, is an island unto himself.**

When you minimize that which I have given you and grasp on to that which is not your natural talent you take precious time away from that which you are called upon to do. Do not fear when you are on track you will be given all of the support, all of the earthly help that you need. **There are others who are part of your mission who are just waiting to use their talents in conjunction with yours.**

Too often My earth angels forget this point and think all falls on their shoulders. Nothing could be farther from the truth. I will send exactly what you need at precisely the right time. There we go with My timing again, yet once you accept this as a fact and have faith I will not leave you, then you can progress easily.

My heavenly angels want you to know and understand they applaud you at this time. You have heard Me say over and over again "When the angels sing?" You have wondered at this saying and now I tell you. When the angels sing in heaven you shall know I return. I caution you do not change these words as you will understand the meaning when the time is right. For now when you hear this singing you will know all is well on this earth and in the heavens (more later).

*My earth angels are all given an opportunity to come to Me of their own volition. Many have been caught up in the myriad of **distractions** which are running rampant in the world today. I tell My children to limit their time on the computer. **I tell my children to stay away from facebook.** You need to know that which works for good can also work for evil. Limit that which can be placed under attack and become a target for the adversary. All of these things which I tell you and My earth angels Wendy, are most important at this time. Anything which becomes a huge distraction My little ones is not of Me. Those distractions **which stifle your talent** and keep you from that which is not of your mission are of Satan and not of the Divine. I can see you are confused at this comment.*

It is not that I do not want My earth angels to have other interests. Often I place other interests in their paths as a conduit for that which they are to accomplish. However, balance in all things is the key. Wendy, use yourself as an example. I know that you have tried to write off and on for a long time now. You have not been successful in that which is My will for you because you were imposing your free will on the subject matter. You were trying to force something that was not in My plan. It was not in the correct order of things. Everything you have written will be shared at some point; be it in the form of a book or in a lecture. Yet, if you only write that which I am telling you at this time, this project will flow effortlessly and you and Jillian will be amazed at the outcome.

There are many who do know their purpose, yet they are floundering. That is the reason for earth angels. *The clergy is often overly cautious regarding that which they feel at a deep level. They are bound to constraints which many of My earth angels are not. You need not be concerned about the elders. Your needs are well provided for therefore you are not held to any specific limitations.* ***You are not subject to the ridicule of man's standards.***

It was not a coincidence I had you watch the news this morning. The young woman who jumped from the bridge into icy waters did so to avoid a semi truck running her over. This is necessary for the reader to understand the sequence of events. While I did not cause the car to slide on the ice, I did stop the car from sliding into the river where she most surely would have been trapped in her vehicle. It was St. Michael who was by her side in the icy waters as she swam for one hour with a broken back. While she was crying for help she soon realized I had heard her petition. Humans can only call this a **miracle** *and of course some give the glory to God. She knew without a doubt she was saved for a purpose and shared this with the media, saying she needed only to find her purpose now. She is an example of one of My earth angels. For she knows without a shadow of a doubt I am there. She will not then have to find her purpose. The purpose will come to her. The purpose has already come. Most often Wendy when an earth angel discovers their purpose it is very apparent. One must not forget I am the conduit. One need only listen and pay attention to that which is around them,* ***that which is of Me. If it is for good, it is for God!***

Listen to the still voice which comes from within. ***That which you hear in the dark gives way in the light*** *(you are thinking of at night when you are in bed). In this instance I am not referring to nightly communion. I am eluding to those moments of darkness when you fear all is lost. I will make Myself known.* ***Mankind lacks faith in huge proportions now My child and must understand the measure of faith is often most apparent in the bleakest moments.***

I use these moments as an opportunity to awaken one's soul. You must, as an earth angel, nurture your soul. My earth angels need to understand the importance of this. When your soul is hungry it will cry out for attention and often will do so in utter despair.

You must take time to make time. *Take time for Me on a daily basis.* **You must make a sanctuary for Me in your home where you can go to spend time with Me if possible.** *Although I reside in each of you finding a sanctuary which is readily accessible will make it easier for you to actively participate in communion with Me. I am present in all things, yet it is important you associate a particular resting spot where you can discern that which is of Me,* **that which I say to you and you alone.**

I have taught you about **Golden Magic Circles** *before and now I want to shed some light on this for My earth angels. Do not limit this circle to those only of a religious nature. Much is to be gleaned from those who attend and those who do not. Rather, look to the heart of each person in your circle and know they are indeed there for a distinct purpose.*

My earth angels need to remember to give thanks in all things. For all things which come to them serve a purpose at this time. This includes not only that which has come in the past but that which is to come in the future. **There is no time for fear in these days and one must put all fear aside** *knowing they are on track with that which they are called to do. Protect that which you write Wendy. Only listen to that which is of the spirit.*

I want to caution you once again about balance so that you remember this should flow effortlessly. I will send you the information you need to do your job. Live in **the moment,** *as that will eliminate all unnecessary* *anxiety. You will then have much joy in that which you are called to do. You will experience joy in writing these pages and know that which I say is the truth. That which I say is indeed the heart of the matter. Do not allow these words to be changed and do not alter them based on other's opinions. If there is something I do not want known it will not be in these pages. There is much to be written of an inspirational nature and even though subjects tend to skip around at this time, you will see how well it all comes together in the end.*

I talk to you now on the subject of heaven for this is a subject that is of most interest to the soul and to the well being of My earth Angels. The world would have you think heaven does not exist in the context you think of. Nothing could be or is farther from the truth. Many of My children have quite a vivid picture of what heaven looks like. These images are not part of the imagination, rather a memory which is housed deep in the confines of one's soul. There are those who have experienced near death episodes and live to tell about what they have seen.

Others of you seem to remember the times in My kingdom. Do not doubt that it is real. Satan would have one think then this is all there is; the thought that heaven is here on earth and there is nothing to look forward to. You have all come from My heavenly realm and you are all under My guidance now. There are those of you who have had encounters with Me on this earth and even having done so have doubted over time it was a real and true experience. This is why I have sent many of you out two by two so that when you become discouraged

you can take solace in knowing another earth angel
has indeed experienced the same thing. For each of you
this encounter could manifest itself in many different
ways. My appearance could be made known in the case
of a miracle such as mentioned earlier. For you it was
a chance encounter in the grocery store. For each of
you it can and may be different according to that which
you are able to accept. Some of you are not comfortable with a face to face encounter with Me. **But one
thing for certain, once you have seen Me, once I
have made myself known you will never be the
same again**. For your soul longs for this communion
and knowing what is the reality and what is the illusion
it longs for that which is of the Divine, for that which it
knows to be the truth.

There is nothing to fear but fear itself. Fear is
not of our Father and keeps one from moving forward
with that which they are called to do. I will always
comfort thee and will come to each of you in a manner
you can and will accept. When I chose My disciples in
the days of long ago I had a purpose. I knew the measure of each of their hearts and knew each would do
that which they were called to do and say on My behalf.
They too had trouble coveting one another for that is
part and parcel of the human element. The important
part then is to be able to recognize when such is the case
and do all one can to keep from getting distracted by
another's talents.

Every person needs encouragement for their gifts
and talents Wendy and that is your job. **You must**

encourage others to express these talents confident they are for the betterment of mankind. *You will be meeting many interesting people in the days and weeks ahead. Encourage them to listen to that which is pulling at their heart strings **and to believe without a shadow of a doubt that which the Divine is calling them to do.** Tell My children to look to the light and the light will surround them. Do not be **distracted by darkness or those things which they have no control over.** For this is a strong tool the adversary uses to make My earth angels believe all is futile. It is time My earthly army recognizes that which is of the adversary and that which is of Me. This book will spell those steps out very clearly for all to read and expose that which is not of Me and that which is of the Divine.*

My earth angels must understand the importance of these words and rejoice for now is the time much is happening. Now is the time when you will be pulled together to accomplish that which is a part of My master plan. This then is a day to rejoice and not to despair. For I am arming all of you with that which you need to do, that which you have been sent to do. Do not worry about the little children Wendy, as they have a great purpose in the years ahead. Do not worry about your family as they are learning at a rapid rate now those things which they are called to do. My earth angels must trust I know their concerns and will see to it all are cared for in My kingdom. Go now and rejoice for this is the day the Lord hath made."

2/16/2011

*"**The secret to living is in the giving.** In the circle of life it is most important one learns this secret. Even for an earth angel this can be most difficult at times. While it is in an earth angel's nature to give often they do not understand the importance of sharing their natural gift and talents. It is important then each understands that which comes naturally to them is of the Father.*

*Part of the challenge for earth angels is you are humble beings at best. This is because you do not naturally respond to the demands of the ego. It is only then as one travels through the journey of life they are thrust into competitive environments which in many cases do not focus on the natural talents one has been blessed with. For many of My earth angels this can be the source of much dis-ease and discontentment **for the soul longs to complete its assigned mission and becomes most impatient over the delays society thrusts at them.***

When one understands the importance of sharing that which comes naturally they relish in the joy of giving. Therefore, as an earth angel you should look closely at the deepest desire of your heart and you will know without a shadow of a doubt that which you are called to do.

Many earth angels are confused by the demands of society. They are thrust into jobs that often keep them from experiencing the joy which was intended for them on this earth. Not all of you will work at jobs which enable you to articulate your gifts. Yet, if you are but listening I will bring to you that which you need to share your gifts with others. **In life then one is meant to learn, to serve and to grow**. For it is in the serving we can share that which we know with others. One then can use any platform to allow the light of Christ to shine through them.

Earth Angels are open to learning. They are able to glean from one another as often I send others to assist one in their mission. Think then of the people who have impacted your life. When you think of the key individuals you will see that which they have contributed to your journey.

Often I will place a most difficult individual in your path for you to see that which you are most challenged by. So you may see that which you do not want to become. As an earth angel you understand there is indeed no room for a critical spirit as each person is on their own personal journey and at different stages of development. **You are there to assist them, to encourage them by your actions and your willingness to share that which you know to be the reality.** That which you know is the true meaning of life.

As an earth angel you have an automatic sense of knowing. You understand life does have a higher purpose. You are thinking there are baby souls in the pecking order of things, of life and you are correct. You *see, one must remember everyone is at various degrees of learning. Think of it then as the school of life.*

There are students and then there are the teachers. **Earth angels are the teachers in the school of life.** *Their credentials consist of those spiritual gifts the heavenly Father bestows upon His children. These spiritual gifts can be articulated any place at any time. Your natural talents may be somewhat restrained but rest assured your spiritual gifts can always be used in the circle of life. I tell you I will always open the door for your natural talents to be shared. You must have faith that this is the case. I am the conductor of life's symphony and you My earth angels are My beautiful musicians. Oh what magnificent music abounds when all is shared with others.*

Do not then fight your purpose. Rather embrace that which you are called to do and be for you are a messenger of God. The circle of life is continuous. In a circle there is no beginning and there is no end and so it is with life. Life then never ends. Your soul never dies. Yet, the health of your soul must be paid attention to. One must listen to the still voice within as it is this voice which is longing to be heard. In nurturing your soul you will blossom into the beautiful flower you were destined to be. You must be the constant gardener of your soul. You must pay attention to what your soul is telling you. If one were to pay as much attention to their soul as to their physical needs they would indeed stay the course.

As an earth angel you will not abandon your principles to obtain that which is of the world. Because you are a messenger of the Divine know then that you are subject to the wiles of Satan. You must guard yourself against the tools of the adversary. The tools of Satan are many. You must guard against distractions. You must take a look at how you spend your time making certain you nurture all aspects of your being. Many of you need to spend more time listening and less time doing those things which are counterpart to your purpose. **When My children spend more time in communion with Me they are not susceptible to depression.** For I alone will comfort you. I will give you that which you need.

I encourage my earth angels to **spend time in nature**. This is the tapestry I have created for all to enjoy. Observe how every living thing has a purpose onto its own. Nothing, absolutely nothing is wasted. You are so precious. You are one of a kind. There is no one else exactly like you. Celebrate your uniqueness! Remember you truly are the greatest gift mankind will ever find! Earth angels need to share this message with all they come in contact with. Whoever is put in your path is indeed an earth angel's responsibility. You must then be a beacon of light for others to follow. I will not fail you for I am always by your side."

2/17/2011

"You have been asking Me many questions. This is good as there is much to be said on the subject of earth angels. You are concerned about who is and who is not an earth angel. This is a discussion of much concern with *the elders in my kingdom, as there are many souls who will do our Father's works in their life time. They will understand their true purpose and the truest meaning of life. All those who come to Me and listen to the callings of the spirit are indeed children of our Father's kingdom.*

There are those on earth at this time who are here to assist others with their life purpose. They are here to help guide them and encourage them to listen to the callings of their soul. My earth angels then are the **cheerleaders** *in the circle of life. They come to this earth with a predetermined understanding of their specific assignment and purpose. This is not to take away from the purpose of all My children who come to me, as many great works will be accomplished by those who listen to the promptings of their soul.*

There will be those who take longer to understand their purpose. There will be those who once they understand their life's purpose choose not to listen to the callings of their soul and then there will be those who will respond with the utmost enthusiasm. These are the ones who then are filled with **holy enthusiasm!** *They will have a never ending supply of energy and joy which will sustain them on their journey. There then is nothing to fear but fear itself. Fear is not of our Father and of course is a strong tool of the adversary. In pursuit then of one's higher purpose My children will be provided with all they need to accomplish that which they are called to do.*

All of My children are given guidance throughout their life time. All of My children have a guardian angel looking over them. These guardians can become most frustrated at times. Yet, they are always there for you, prompting you, watching you and protecting you from the adversary.

You are asking Me Wendy about the definition of earth angels and do not want to discourage or minimize the importance of others. If you listen to my words this will be written for all to understand and they indeed will be motivated to their higher purpose. If all then were earth angels there would be naught to accomplish the many other myriad of tasks which need attending to.

When all come together in the name of our Father, when all let go of the many deterrents the ego is capable of, My kingdom will reign on this earth. In the Father's kingdom all work for Me. All have different assignments and all have different tasks to complete. The same is on earth. All of My children are given that which they need to accomplish their higher purpose. Some will choose not to listen. Even if they do listen they will choose not to acknowledge this inner longing is indeed of the Divine.

*It is never too late to come to the Father. I am most concerned of course about each of your souls as I love all of My children with an intensity you cannot fully understand. Many complain it would be far easier had they not been given the gift of **free will**. Yet, this is a necessary component in a soul's development. Free will is the catalyst for each soul's lesson plan. This free will enables one to focus on that which each soul needs to attain the desired state of enlightenment they are working* towards. **Free will is to the soul as the Holy Spirit is to the Divine.**

There are in each person's life those **AH-HA moments one experiences as a catalyst in the development of the soul**. These are pivotal moments in each person's life. These moments provide one with an opportunity to grasp that which they need to know, that which is needed to understand one's mission in life. These AH-HA moments one should reflect on as they are moments which will have a soulful impact on one's journey. The AH-HA moments most often then will alter or change the pathway one has been on to date.

It is the gleaning of these moments one will see a clear picture of what and how their mission is to be accomplished. It is for some like putting pieces of a puzzle together. One should meditate on the AH-HA moments as they are most important. These moments are guided by the Divine Compass.

An earth angels understands, there is no such thing as coincidence and therefore encourages others to embrace these moments. **These coincidences to an earth angel are God incidences indeed.**

These pivotal moments in life often can be most painful, yet they provide the turning point which allows one to reach a higher understanding of life. **God incidences provide an opportunity to connect with one's higher purpose. These AH-HA moments most often bring about waves of compassion which provide the passion needed**

to move forward with one's higher purpose. *That is why one should give thanks in all things. For it is in the closing of one door another one opens. Nothing is wasted in God's kingdom. No experience should be wasted in one's life. The adversary would use these experiences to pull one away from the Divine, yet these very same experiences are the ones which can lead us closer to joy.*

Through sorrow comes joy. An earth angel understands the important role sorrow plays towards the attainment of enlightenment. One cannot fully appreciate one without the other. Often those experiences which lay heavy on the heart are the same experiences which lead us towards a more joyful and meaningful way of life. We then must ask the Lord to help us see through His eyes what He sees. He will help us then to understand what is to be gained by this experience. Earth angels need to help others through these times of sorrow so they may embrace the joy which comes from a higher awareness only the Divine can give. It is through this awareness the true meaning of life is given clarity. Those things then of the world do take on an entirely different meaning and importance. It is often through sorrowful experiences one begins to understand the difference between joy and sorrow.

It is therefore crucial one understands, in these times of economic unrest, that which manifests joy. This is when one must clearly define for themselves the principles of joy."

2/19/2011

"Earth angels know they have a responsibility to share their God given talents with one another. They cannot take this responsibility lightly as there are many who depend on that which they are called to do. It will not be the same for every one, yet all will be God's messengers on earth.

In the world today there is a great aura of complacency. There are many who know yet have been sorely tested. I have promised My chosen shall not fail. Those who know Me shall be rewarded in My kingdom for completing the tasks they have been called to do. The more time then you spend in communion with Me the more you will hear the words of encouragement you need. For how can there be cheerleaders without a coach?

You understand from whence you come and therefore need to spend more time with that which is the reality not that which is the illusion. Although you are here on earth with all of its many distractions and temptations to be balanced and gain the strength you will need in the days to come, you must spend time with Me!

There are many of you who attend church on a regular basis and there are just as many who do not. Either way this is not a prerequisite for being an earth angel. Yet, you must cultivate and nourish our relationship as I have said before. You must build the confidence you need to fully trust that which you are hearing in communion with Me. Many of you have difficulty with this as you are so consumed with the rigors of life and that which is not the reality you doubt that which you hear. **Practice! Practice! Practice!** You will build your confidence in this manner. Truly you cannot learn this any other way than by spending time with Me.

An earth angel works directly for Me and cannot do what he or she is called to do if they do not have an active relationship with the Divine. This relationship is the most important relationship you have, therefore, why do some of you spend so little time with Me? Why do you allow yourselves to doubt? Even those who have seen Me doubt. Where then is your faith? **Faith moves mountains. You, as an earth angel, can move mountains through Me if you but allow Me to guide you.** If you but trust in the words that are written. This book is written especially for you My little ones. Trust that this is the case and you will be renewed. These words will speak in a different manner to each of you as there is something here for everyone.

When I say **be not humble in My regard** you simply need to move forward with that which is your God given talent. **You will know that talent by the ease in which it flows.** If indeed it feels as though you are going against the tide then you know this is not what you are called to do. For when you use your gifts for Me there is much joy in the work you do. You will be filled with a new surge of energy! You will be given all that you need to complete your part of the assignment. Often there will be more than one involved in an assignment.

You need only concern yourself with the part you are called to do. You must be willing to allow others to contribute that which is their gift.

When one then works together in harmony with others so much more can be accomplished. When one works together in harmony miraculous works can and will take place. It will be as though the mission is infused with power. **As this harmony produces an energy that cannot be harnessed. A sure sign of the adversary is discord. Whenever discord is abound, conflict, arguments and dissension always prevail. What great works can manifest in this type of environment? In doing the works of our Father then harmony is a sure sign one has stayed the course. It is a sure sign our Father's will is evident.**

As earth angels you are called to bring harmony to that which is not of the Father. You then are called upon to use your gifts for the betterment of others. That which has been given freely by our Father should indeed manifest in those who work for Me. If you are cast in a situation where your light cannot shine, where darkness prevails, then you must listen to that which the spirit is telling you to do. There will be those times when you will need to shake the dust from your feet as in the days of old and let the spirit guide you elsewhere. This does not mean that you have failed! It simply means it is time to move elsewhere. I know the goodness of one's heart. I will not allow you to waste your time now on a heart *that is closed to the Divine. That is for Me to take care of. There will be other doors which will open for I will not allow My work to be hindered for any reason. If it is of good, it is of God. Then My works shall be accomplished!*

We have talked about God's timing, we have talked about the importance of communing with our heavenly Father, we have talked about harmony and now we must talk about that which is to come.

*I do not want My chosen to be consumed with that which is of the future. I **do not** want you to focus on future events. Much the same as I do not want you to lament over the past. For the past cannot be changed and as we have discussed much that has happened in the past has led you to where you are today. The past then was part of your lesson plan. You cannot control the future, you cannot predict the future. **Only our heavenly Father knows what will happen at any precise moment**. That has never been for My children to know. Yet, know this, the future is in My hands. **Much can be altered by what transpires moment to moment.** I am watching all of mankind now as they respond to many attacks from the adversary. What I can tell you is that the adversary will not win, of that you can be very certain. So what I ask of My children is to focus on the here and now. **I ask that you live in the moment**. This way My little ones you will harness all of the energy needed for the immediate task at hand. Do you understand the importance of this? By focusing on the moment you will see through My eyes that which you need to see. You will hear that which you* *need to hear. One must be on full alert now. You see My little one, I have just given you the tool in which to fight complacency with. **For when you are fully engaged in the moment you can clearly see that which is important!** You then will act on that which you are called to do.*

*   ***Every time one connects with another human being it is their responsibility to share that which they know with one another. One therefore must be fully engaged in the moment.** No man knows the hour I will come and no man shall know how or where I shall appear. I do not mean to be redundant on this subject yet this is most important. **One then must be fully present in the moment. This is a key tool against the adversary!***

*   *As an earth angel you will know that which you need to know at the precise moment. It is key then you listen to that which I am saying to each of you. **Do not let a day go by without communing with Me. I have never asked this of you before but now you must listen! I am your Father and will always take care of you. I have formed a covenant with thee and this covenant shall not be broken.** You must trust that each of you is being guided at this time."*

2/20/2011

*   *"I am pleased to see your enthusiasm Wendy. I am filling you with My spirit as you are so willing to do that which I am calling you to do. You are indeed My faithful*

servants and the angels in heaven are singing now. There are many in heaven dancing with joy for they are now seeing the results they have been praying for. Do not take these words out little one for they are of Me.

You were surprised to read last night "right and mindful decisions" in the Buddhist sense means to live in the moment. It was fun to see the look on your face little one and I am anxious to see the look on Jillian's face as well when she reads this. I will always confirm you are on track. You need not fear My faithful servant. Do you see how important it is to be in balance little one? This is crucial for My earth angels to understand. When you are balanced one can look forward with joy completing the work I have called you to do. I want My children to flourish and live a life filled with joy. That then means nurturing all aspects of your being.

What now you need to understand and teach many is the importance of nurturing their soul. For when the soul is nurtured all else comes into fruition. As My earth angels know the soul is the most important part of one's being. Yet, Satan uses so many tactics to keep one from acknowledging the important role one's soul plays in the journey of life. The hungry soul longs for communion with Me. The hungry soul wants to converse, it is crying out in the night to be heard. Yet, still so many of My children are not truly listening. They speak but they do not hear. When you are still, you will hear that which you need to hear. When you live in the moment you can focus on that which I am telling you for

to be in the moment means to limit distractions.
When one lives in the moment they are able to nurture
all aspects of their being as they do not waste needless
energy on that which they cannot control. This then is
the key to insuring all aspects of your being flourish.

When it seems as though some of your writings are
repetitive you will see there, indeed is a reason for this.
Simply write and you will enjoy the process and be
amazed at the overall result!

I have mentioned **healistic and holistic**. While
there is no word yet known to man as healistic it will be
used for the means of comparison. I wish you and others
to understand. Much time and energy is devoted toward
healing. Many who study healing focus on the disease
rather than the dis-ease of the individual who is ill.

Cancer does indeed run rampant in the United States.
While scientists have found cancer does have to do
with one's DNA, in other words it runs in families, they
disregard the spiritual state and emotional state of the
families that seem to succumb to this disease generation upon generation. This is a very complex subject for
many. In order to understand this disease, one need then
reflect on their own family patterns and history. Do not
look at the physical aspect rather look at the emotional
pattern of one's family. What balance and order in the
journey of life was practiced generation to generation?
How much time was spent nourishing the soul? When
one is in direct communion with our heavenly Father
they listen to that which comes from within. They then

are able to ward off much of the dis-ease which comes from lack of understanding and harmony in one's life. When one is not at peace or surrounded by discord, this causes a major breakdown in the immune system. To start then the healing process there must be a holistic approach to healing versus the healistic approach, as all aspects of one's being need to be nurtured in order for balance to be restored.

If you reflect on this My little one you will understand very much. Western civilization has had a difficult time understanding and accepting the concept of meditation. They have a difficult time understanding the pecking order of things. For without this balance there cannot be true health or lasting health of any nature. When one then looks inward rather than at the exterior they are able to understand many things. They are able to heal that which has been the catalyst for disease to attack. I know this is a subject you do not enjoy, yet it is key to helping others through the difficult periods in one's life.

My earth angels are often asked if I cause bad things to happen to people. More important they phrase the question, "Why do bad things happen to good people?" First and foremost let Me address something that has been troubling Me for a very long time. **I do not cause bad things to happen to any of My children.** *My children are given the freedom to choose that which they cultivate in their life. They can either choose to listen to the spirit and acknowledge that from whence they come or they can choose not to listen to the spirit. That is up to each and every one of you. This is My will for*

My children. I want them to come to Me of their own volition. They must arrive at this choice on their own. When they accept Me and understand the love I have for them they can be assured I am always there for them. Your earthly bodies are a temporary condition. They are a necessary part of the human experience. It then is your soul I am most concerned about as your soul lives throughout eternity. **Therefore, it is prudent one learn the importance of the soul versus the body which is merely temporal.**

Your earthly bodies then were not meant to last forever. Some life spans indeed are shortened through one's own behavior and practices. In many cases I allow certain events to take place so My children will sit up and pay attention to that which is endangering their spiritual path, that which is keeping them from understanding their higher purpose. Often these setbacks afford one the time to listen to that which their soul has been trying to tell them. Always remember it is the soul I am most concerned about. I and I alone know the **heart of the matter,** *that which truly needs to be healed. For once this clarity has taken place each is able then to proceed on the right path which will allow them to complete their earthly mission.*

There are those who have been assigned a specific purpose. This may necessitate a shorter life span. While humans call this predestination it is merely a matter of accomplishing their assigned mission on earth. These soul's know that which they have been called to do and are most anxious to complete their task, they then are *filled with **holy enthusiasm**. In the case of the young they are indeed wrapped in the arms of their guardian angels. They are surrounded by heavenly beings. Heavenly beings who are waiting to escort them to our Father's kingdom. My true believers understand death is a most necessary part of life. Death cannot be avoided in the world as you know it today. Help others then understand the circle of life. Help them look upon death as a stepping stone in the order of life. **The completion of one's earthly journey is merely a process in the cycle of eternity. It is a necessary part of the learning process.***

***Predestination is not the same as fatalism!** If this were the case the power of prayer would be obsolete in requests for healing of the sick! **Fatalism limits the power of the Divine.** A vast majority of adversities are indeed a direct result of one's free will. Many humans simply say when your time is up your time is up. **Be careful in limiting the power of prayer for often I use these difficult circumstances as an opportunity to make known my presence to many!** In the case then of a miraculous healing it is not one's time for they have not completed their life purpose. Those then who refer to fatalism indeed need to spend more time in communion with Me as I will give them the answers they seek.*

*To say that everyone does not have a purpose is like saying the sun or moon has no purpose. All living things have a purpose! All things created serve a purpose. **Our Father has a purpose for all things!***

Some of My earth angels work with the sick and the dying. *Guard against those thoughts then the adversary would have you think. Focus on the circle of life and the purpose of all things. For the circle of life to be complete one must then complete their life's journey on earth. When My children cease to learn, cease to serve and cease to grow there is naught to be gained by remaining on this earth. Some live long lives on earth to be given every possible opportunity to come to Me. To be given every possible opportunity to make amends with those they love.* **To forgive and be forgiven** *is part and parcel in the circle of life. Forgiveness is a necessary criteria for passage to heaven. For it is through the act of forgiveness we are free to continue on in our quest towards enlightenment. One cannot afford to harbor ill will towards another. One cannot harbor a* **critical spirit**. *For this lesson will be learned one way or the other.* **The importance of forgiveness then is the pathway to the Divine."**

2/21/2011

"You are most enthusiastic now My little one. You see this need not be cumbersome. Simply listen in the still of the night and it will give light in the day! There is so much to be said and for the purpose of earth angels I am touching on the subjects I feel are of primary importance in the days and weeks ahead.

While My earth angels know basic truths there are key points I want all of you to focus on now at this time. We have talked about healistic

versus holistic. We have talked about balance in all things, living in the moment and the importance of harmony. We have briefly talked about the tools of complacency and distraction which Satan is using in dynamic proportions in these days.

I will address many things in the days to come, yet I want you to understand in no uncertain terms the importance of what is transpiring on earth at this time. There are many of My children who have felt at dis-ease for a very long time. Yet, due to the rigors of life and the daily demands which are placed on all they have allowed themselves to become **victims of society**. This of course is the result of the adversary and keeps My children from experiencing the full measure of My joy. They are so distracted and so busy being busy they do not listen to that which is coming from the interior.

All of My children have been blessed with natural gifts and talents. It is so important that you as my earth angels impress this upon My children. No one comes to earth without My blessings. **What kind of a Father would I be if I did not equip My children with the natural tools they would need to accomplish that which is their mission on earth?** Over the past several decades greed has become a prominent consideration in one's livelihood. Many times parents have encouraged their children to pursue an education or major which would not enhance or utilize their natural gifts and talents. There is an earthly saying which says, "Do what you love and the money will follow." **As your**

Father in heaven I say do that which comes from the heart, that which you are most enthusiastic about and you will indeed be filled with joy. For all humans have a responsibility to share their natural gifts and talents. In fact their soul longs for them to give unconditionally that which is of the Divine. When humans understand the importance of listening to that which they are called to do they will indeed experience true joy on earth. Satan does of course not want these gifts to be shared. For when one is filled with passion for that which they do there are no conditions or strings attached. **There is no hidden agenda**. For one derives a great deal of pleasure pursuing that which comes from the heart.

When one enjoys the task at hand they do not experience the stress which is so prevalent in the world today. They in fact have a never ending flow of energy. When one listens to the spirit they are able to balance all aspects of life as they trust our heavenly Father will see to all of their needs. **When one is forced to do that which does not come naturally the soul is most anxious**.

It is most crucial then as earth angels you encourage all to follow their heart. For some they would say follow their dreams. If they but learn to trust their inner instincts all will be well. When man learns this important truth peace will abound on earth. When you see all the unrest and disharmony in the world today it is most apparent there are many who are not utilizing their natural gifts and talents.

There is much disharmony in the world today, a world that is driven primarily on the standards of man, **a world that is dictated by the ego.** *One then needs to develop their inner sense to know that which is indeed the reality.*

For a long time now I have allowed My earth angels to direct their attention to earthly matters. I have seen how difficult it can be for all of you living in the world when your spirit is not of the world. Now I ask you spend more time with Me. I ask that you focus on that which is the true reality. When you do so, you will find peace in the days and weeks ahead.

Do you remember Wendy when I told you I wanted you to teach others to go to the cave within? I am showing you now that which needs to be taught so others will understand the importance and benefit of nurturing their souls. One cannot do that which they do not understand. I need all of My children now to pay attention. They will have all of the answers and tools they need in the days and months ahead if they but listen and understand that which is the reality, that which is of the Divine.

Let events unfold as they may in this world. **Only concern yourselves with the moment and each of you will be able to complete and understand the task at hand. My children need to understand from whence they come. Satan would have My children believe this is a fallacy, this is the illusion. Yet, one only need look to nature to understand creation. I will give each of you the**

necessary words to say at the appropriate times.
I will send you where I want you to go. I will not
waste your talents or your loyalty to me.

When you have faith in your heavenly Father and
acknowledge He is all knowing and He indeed knows the
measure of each of your hearts, you then simply need to
cultivate that which is already yours to share.

You ask Me Wendy where, when and how can you
teach these truths? This guide book is to encourage My
children now to spend more time with Me. They need
to know the answers they seek are already there. **Very**
often then the answer you seek lies in the ques-
tion itself. For it is in the questioning we become
aware of that which is one's higher purpose.

You as My little ones need to keep abreast of what
is happening in the world, yet do not allow yourself to
spend unnecessary time dwelling on that which you
cannot control. **Rather take the time you spend**
casting your eyes on the media and cast your
eyes on that which is of the Divine.

I will give you the answers you seek My little one.
The media is a tool used by the adversary to
keep one from living in the moment, to keep one
from acting on that which they are called to do
each and every day.

Music is tonic for the soul. It is so much better to
listen to the talents of My people rather than listen to
the batting of gums. Many news casters allow their

ego to dictate that which they report. They thrive on sensationalism rather than that which is the truth. Earth angels understand bad news indeed travels twice as fast as good news. The internet now is being used in ways that cause great unrest. It is not that communication is bad. It is just that there are too many who would use this means of communication to influence those who fall prey to the wiles of Satan. Satan uses the media to instill fear and a sense of hopelessness.

Ask then our heavenly Father to guide you in all endeavors now. He will help you to discern that which is the truth and that which is not. **Concern yourself then with that which is in the realm of your capabilities. In doing so you will have a positive and holy effect on those you connect with**. Be then a beacon of light for all you connect with. Do not be a conduit of darkness. When there are days you feel less than enthusiastic come to Me and I will restore your holy enthusiasm. I want to be able to use you for the betterment of mankind. I want you to share your gifts with one another.

Happiness is fleeting, as events, people, places and things are constantly changing. One thing for certain is change. The lasting joy one seeks comes from within. It comes from understanding the true measure of life. The answers and assurance one seeks are not found in religion. They are found by establishing a relationship with our heavenly Father. **For some, religion acts as a conduit for prayer**. It is the introduction to what is possible. Yet, the only way to understand the full measure of life is through a personal relationship with the Divine.

Religion then is not for everyone. Yet, it is a place of worship for many. It is a place to connect with those who are seeking a relationship with the Divine. Therefore, never discourage my children from pursuing a church home. Rather encourage them into a deeper understanding of that which is needed to truly be in communion with the Divine.

One then must not have a critical spirit in this regard. There are so many of My children who are in need of comfort. There are so many of My children who are experiencing a great deal of dis-ease and unrest in these times. Many of My earth angels are able to reach out in ways those of the cloth cannot. You therefore must be careful in your actions understanding you have a holy job to do. You must act in a manner which is worthy of our heavenly Father. Simply understand there are eyes on you now observing your actions. The opposition is watching how you respond to various life challenges at this time. You have heard the expression actions speak louder than words; there indeed is much to be said for this. For Satan cannot know your thoughts but most certainly is aware of your actions, your response and the words you speak. **He indeed will strike at that which is your greatest weakness**. Whenever you are the closest to accomplishing that which is of the Divine the adversary is on full alert. When under attack simply lift up a prayer asking for protection. You will be filled with the power of the Holy Spirit. Your fears will be dispelled. **Meditate on fear and you will come to understand fear is often the basis for wrong action**. *Fear often causes then one to react to a situation rather than respond with that which is of the Divine.*"

2/24/2011

"When one gets religiosity out of the way, is willing to share their natural gifts and talents with all and sheds that which is of the ego, true joy shall manifest on this earth. Therefore, I tell you do not covet the gifts of one another. Rather come together in harmony. **Come together with a common purpose and you will be the forerunners, the catalyst to a new kingdom on this earth**. You wrote cover a moment ago. Think then about the different meaning between cover and covet. Do not think one gift is more important than the other. Do not hold power over another nor limit the importance of each individual task. You must be careful not to limit the gifts of one another. True earth angels encourage one another to participate in the common good. In this manner My light shall be luminescent of all. You each play an integral part in these works. Therefore, I caution you, think only of that which you are called to do. Be not humble in My regard yet be humble in the part you play. **It is in the coming together of all the parts which indeed is the answer for all**.

Do not sit in judgment of one another. Too often My children place themselves in the role of judge and jury. I am the judge of each of you. I am the jury. Rather pray for holy understanding. Pray for right minded thinking and this shall come. It will be as though you have a new wisdom and clarity in which to see things and circumstances as never before.

I who have created the world created you! You are My shining stars in the darkest of nights. Look at the stars of the night and see the brilliance when all come together. A single star gives light, yet when many come together they become a beacon of light for all to see even in the darkest of nights. Such is the coming together of man's gifts and talents. This is the way it is in our Father's kingdom and is My desire that this should manifest on this earth. This is the way to seek the peace which will and can surpass all human understanding to date.

Take heed to these words then, do not take lightly that which you are called to do. Do not minimize your gifts as they are intended to contribute to that of the greater good for all! You must then think with a new mind. You must act on that which is of the spirit with confidence! When you come together with this mind set then there will be much clarity of purpose. **There will be a common renewal intended for these times**. I will show you the correct way to influence, to alter that which is in the making. You shall be My holy warriors, My earth angels. For you are armed with the Holy Spirit. Do not doubt this is the case! Have faith My little ones in that which is being written to date. Do not allow room for doubt. I will send those of like minds to all of you and much will be accomplished.

Encourage those around you to try new things and be willing to open their minds to that which they never thought possible before. Many times My children are unaware of that which they are capable of, closing their minds off to new possibilities.

When things do not flow as one would anticipate, pray for right understanding of that which they are trying to accomplish. I will help My children to understand, to see that which they need to move forward with the task at hand. I will send the people who will be eager to assist them in their mission.

Think back on the key people in each of your lives and you will see this has always been the case for each of you. Help others to see this has always been the case for each of My children. You all need each other My child. Many times the ego causes one to set themselves above one another. This never serves the higher good. Look at the world to date and you will see this type of thinking only limits and sets one against one another. You must love with the heart of our Father.

Embrace one another as I embrace you. This is not as easy to put into practice as one would think. Yet, I tell you if one but appreciates and embraces one another for the gifts they have been given, then much can be accomplished for the greater good of all. There are many "critical spirits" in your world today. **These poor souls are imbued with fear.** I see you researching the word imbued! It is most appropriate in this context little one as these souls are saturated with such a deep and abiding fear they are unable to serve as intended. **They are limiting not only their own potential** *for right understanding but the potential of all those they connect with as well.*

I want to talk about the ego versus the longings of the spirit; those gentle nudges which come from the depths of one's soul. My children have been taught throughout their journey to respond to the dictates of mankind. They have been taught to look for that which they need from exterior forces. **Often, My children blindly trust that which society dictates as the absolute truth**. I find this most interesting as only the Divine can truly know the measure of another's heart. Why is it then mankind has become so complacent? Why is it then mankind only questions when it suits his immediate purpose? For many it is a matter of convenience, the easy way out. For others it is simply to do otherwise would not afford them the liberties they so readily embrace. While this is part and parcel of the human condition it is also a great tool of the adversary; **to entice one to focus on those things which limit the soul's potential to achieve that which is one's true purpose;** to achieve that which cultivates joy in each and every person's life. The soul will always serve as your compass, if you listen to the gentle nudging from within. Yet, you must limit those distractions which keep you from listening to that which the spirit is saying to each of you.

Be careful you decipher that which is of the spirit then and that which is of man. I will always give you the answers you seek. This is why I say over and over you must spend time with Me. I will always confirm that *which I desire. You must live in the moment to know that which I am saying. You then will not miss the important signs which you are each being given. If I do not want something I will show you. of this you can be certain. When you listen there will be clarity and no room for doubt. TRUST, TRUST and TRUST!"*

2/25/2011

"Now listen carefully Wendy as this is most important for all earth angels to teach! **One must take time to make time.** *This statement is very simple, yet so often not practiced in the world today. Many of My children have been spinning their wheels for a very long time. Although they long to experience a more fulfilling way of life they limit their choices using a lack of time as the excuse. If one were to truly spend time reflecting on how each moment is spent they would find there indeed would be time for all. You cannot change that which you do not acknowledge.* **Once you understand how you fill your moments you can then alter your current schedule to accommodate that which brings you and others joy.** *For some this is merely a shift in priorities. Upon reflection there will be those who will need to make some major changes in their life. These major changes often will be predicated by an AH-HA moment in one's life. These moments provide one with an opportunity to become the beautiful person they were created to be. They are the catalyst for change. A change their soul has been longing to be made for some time.*

When you understand one is sent here to learn, to serve and to grow it is imperative one pay attention to all three of these requirements. *There are no free rides in life My little ones. There is always a consequence for each and every action. That is why it is so important to practice right mindfulness at all times. These consequences have a spiral effect on those we connect with. That is why it is crucial to remind others of the tremendous responsibility each has for one another. When you see a soul that is in distress treat them as I would treat you. They are put in your pathway for a distinct reason. You are to learn from all things for this is the essence of life. Perhaps, one is meant to learn to be more compassionate, tolerant or forgiving. Whatever you are meant to learn you will know if you ask the Divine to guide you.* ***One often learns from that which is less than lovely in our eyes***. *Often those who give one the most discomfort are a mirror reflecting that which is less than lovely about oneself. When this is the case then use this as an opportunity to alter that which is causing you distress.*

When one changes that within oneself they then change the way they see others as well. They then are able to practice increased waves of compassion knowing all are a continuous work in progress, be it earth angel or not. When one no longer learns they limit the magnitude of life. Do not then be frightened by that which you do not understand, rather pray for understanding. For how can you teach or combat that which you do not understand? When man increases his

*knowledge he is able to gain wisdom from the experi-
ence this knowledge brings. There then are no negative
experiences as all experience is opportunity for growth.
It is through this new growth one then is able to **serve**
to fullest capacity. How wonderful to know one has
been given the necessary tools they need to serve one
another. One should not question the gift they have been
given, but simply or more aptly put accept the gift they
have been given. Once they have fully accepted this
gift then man must simply be willing to share his gifts
with others! "For you truly are the best present
mankind will ever find."*

2/26/2011

*"My little one, what you write now you must not think
too hard on and please do not change the words as all
will become clear at a later date. I have talked about
covering one another's gifts and I have talked about
coveting one another's gifts and now I want to talk
about the coming together of gifts.*

*You must remember perception is not truth and you
must understand and teach other's My purpose may not
always be apparent. You must be willing now to be open
vessels and listen to that which the spirit is calling you to
do. Often My true purpose is not apparent initially, yet if
one is willing to listen to what the spirit is leading them
to do you will understand all, of this you can be certain.*

*When two or more are gathered in the name of the
Divine many great things are possible. Yet, one needs
then to understand the workings of the Divine as well*

as the workings of the ego. For the ego's first interest is of self, where as our Father's interest is of all. Many Divine opportunities are missed because of the ego and of course the standards of man. That is to say how mankind values one's self worth.

When one then is willing to look at a particular situation through the eyes of the Divine they are able to understand the true purpose of the task. When you trust, you are able to enjoy the process rather than the end result; you are able to see through the eyes of a child, with the innocence of a child recognizing one gift, one talent is no greater than another's. You will be filled with enthusiasm knowing there is something to be gained from everyone!

In working for the Divine then My little one it is imperative one learn to enjoy the process. When you enjoy the process you then become open vessels for Divine creation. Teach this My little one. Teach others to focus on the immediate moment allowing creative energy to flow.

How often does man catch himself thinking about the end result rather than the moment at hand? How often does one consume their thoughts with feelings of inadequacy? In order to overcome these feelings, in order to embrace the moment one must disregard the prompting of the ego. One must understand how unique each person is. One must understand no two people ultimately think alike, see things alike, nor do they act exactly alike. Beauty then is in the eye of the beholder. **I am asking My children then to be open vessels.** I am asking *you to share that which is uniquely of you. I am asking you to have an appreciation for the gifts you have been given and be willing to* **expose** *that which is then your natural gifts and talents.*

I want My children to expand their horizons. I do not want them to be closed to all that is around them. **For in the coming together of talents, by opening oneself to one another's talents you will be able to see clearly the greater good!** *You will see possibilities you never imagined possible before. You will see the greater good which can be accomplished.*

Mankind often has a hidden agenda as your government has a hidden agenda. In My kingdom there is no hidden agenda. All is open for others to see. All work for the common good of one another and there is much joy. There are no fleeting moments of happiness. My children's gifts are readily shared with one another.

I am preparing the way for My kingdom to reign on earth. *I am teaching you now a higher understanding, a holy understanding.* **While in theory this seems as though the coming together of one's gifts and talents should be a simple task, it is indeed the most difficult of all. Until all of My children understand then the true meaning of life and the responsibility they have for one another your world today cannot change.** *For all to know the true joy which is possible man must listen now to that which the Divine is saying. You must settle down the chaotic thoughts of the mind and listen to that which comes from the center of one's being. Do not* spend needless energy on that which does not now serve the common good. I have and am giving each of you the tools you need to come together in these days. Be not afraid to expose that which is of your higher nature. Be not afraid to face your fears, for fear is not of the Divine and I shall help you abate those fears. You must now understand the importance of responding to your higher nature. You must know all is being prepared for those who open their hearts to Me.

You must be aware of those tools which the adversary will use to keep you from your purpose. **I am there for you and when you feel you are under attack I will protect you**. Be on alert for those tools which keep you focusing on that which is of the ego, from focusing on that which robs you then of your true joy! I love all of you so very much and want you to understand the importance of these times. I do not want you to be filled with discouragement and remorse. For often when it seems as though nothing is going right, as though nothing is working, be patient as this is when much work is being done! Do not limit My potential. Do not limit My plans for each of you. Have trust and faith I do know your concerns and that I do know the deepest measure of your hearts. Take heed as I am your Father in heaven. I know all about you and your trials. My way is the kingdom to heaven. Keep your eyes and your heart on the Divine My children and you will experience the fruits of your labor.

I cannot make Myself known to you if you are not living in the moment. This will keep you from focusing on that which is not of Me. This will keep those thoughts at bay which bring My children such unrest and dismay. Have I not provided for all of you to date? Is there not food on your table and a roof over your head? I understand for many these have been very difficult times. Yet, I am there for you and will see you through the most severe trials. **I will always show you another way. I will always bring to you what you need at precisely the right time**.

"The Lord is my shepherd I shall not want, He maketh me lie down in green pastures, and yea though I walk through the valley of the shadow of death I shall fear no evil, **as Thy rod and Thy staff comfort me!**" I ask My children to reflect on these words as they are written, for truly I say to you I am always there for each and every one of you. **Whenever you feel the farthest away from Me I am the closest!**

I want My children to experience a true and lasting joy. I want them to understand the true meaning of life. I have given you the gift of free will and now I am asking you to pay attention to the Divine will. As your Father I want then what is best for you. I need you to pay attention to that which your soul is guiding you to. I want you to understand how little truly is in your control now. The way to the Father is through Me. You always have a choice, yet understand I as your heavenly Father have no hidden agenda. My only agenda is My unconditional love for you. I am not trying to put limits on your life or

your world as you know it today. I am trying now to awaken you to all that is truly at your disposal if you only but listen to that which is the reality. I have all the answers you seek. I do not wish to impose meaningless limits. Rather, I want you to cultivate that which has always been intended for My children."

2/27/2011

Last night, Jesus, you continued to talk to me about laughter. Laughter You say is a tonic for the soul and **exemplifies a joy filled heart**! I find it most interesting You talk to me about laughter as You know how much Jillian and I both enjoy a good laugh. What is it then I can tell others about laughter?

*"In the absence of laughter My little one there is a formidable force at work. Laughter is a gift from our heavenly Father and denotes that which is the response of a child. **It produces endorphins which indeed enhance one's energy and is contagious. It is a positive contagion and is a natural response.***

This is more important than you realize because when one can indeed rejoice in the moment it is a formidable tool against the adversary. The sign of a joyful soul is one who understands the benefit of laughter and readily calls on this most joyful response. The sign of laughter is a natural response and intended to be shared with others.

In the world today you hear less and less laughter. This is because far too many of My children are bogged down living a life which is full of disharmony and chaos. This is a chaos which can be altered no matter what conditions one may be surrounded by. The lack of a joyful heart is a heart which carries far too many burdens. It is a heart which does not trust in that which is the reality and it is a heart which has been hardened to that which is of the Divine. As earth angels you must teach those around you, remind those around you, **the absence of laughter is indeed a significant warning something is amiss.**

Many times in today's world I hear people comment on the lack of friendliness and warmth displayed to one another. This is a condition which can be changed so easily. If My children would but lay their burdens at My feet their spirits would indeed be lifted. A smile is contagious and often opens the most hardened of hearts. It provides a conduit for conversation. It is an open invitation to participate in new relationships. Perhaps, a relationship which will bring one much delight and comfort. The adversary wants each of you to feel isolated and alone in your troubles. The only time the adversary encourages coming together is for the intense purpose of social and economic unrest. Do you see where I am going with this?

Many times I have said mankind is indeed responsible for one another. In the absence of laughter, a warm smile or cordial greeting you have closed yourselves off to many opportunities and soulful connections! I am not asking any of you to be that which you are not. I am merely asking each of you to look at your own behaviors in this regard. There is so much man can change in their immediate surroundings if you but listen to that which the Divine is saying.

You did not think or see where the subject of laughter would go last night My little one. Now do you see what the message is about? I ask only that you trust that what comes to you and I will share that which is intended for all. These key points are to be included in the book. You are beginning to see a format now. Do not get ahead of yourself little one as this is your biggest challenge. You and Jillian need to remember Satan knows your biggest weaknesses so merely remember to live in the moment. Pay close attention to what I am telling the two of you and all will be well. All is well.

Wendy there is no greater thing in the world than love. **Love is the anecdote which can and will cure all.** When mankind is willing to truly open his heart to one another you will be closer to My kingdom on this earth. Years ago I told you to analyze the Lord's Prayer. Focus on "Thy kingdom come, Thy will be done." For when you are living in the will of our heavenly Father He will give you the tools you need to persevere. He will help you get back on track to that which will help you accomplish that which you have been called to do.

I have been talking to you about exercising one's creative side of their brain. You have been asking Me My thoughts on this and wanting to know what to tell others in this regard. From the standpoint of the soul **when one exercises the creative side of their brain it provides a conduit to the soul. Creative energy** *is very different than mindful energy. Creative energy then flows from the center of ones being, from the very deepest part of each of My children. This is such a beautiful part of each of you and as you progress in the world this must be protected and exercised! Now you understand when I talked to you about the art class as an exercise. It is a means, a conduit, to get back in touch with one's creative side.* **This then is nourishment for one's soul and will indeed increase one's soulful activities.**

There is so much to be shared with all and it requires one to shift their thoughts from that of mankind to that which is of the spirit. All of My children are capable of so very much more. Over the next few days and weeks I will be showing all of you how to unmask that which is not of the spirit and become open vessels of the Divine. It is not as difficult as one may think and simply requires an open heart. **Many humans would say an open mind, but the heart is the key.**

Wendy, you are filled with enthusiasm because you have once again opened your heart to that which the spirit is saying to you. Jillian is filled with enthusiasm as well. You now are on the right track to accomplish that which I have called you to do.

It is imperative you surround yourself by those thoughts which come from the center of your being. While the subjects I am calling you to write about seem so simple and obvious, surely, you see now the **subtleties of the adversary.** *Simply reflect on that*

which I am saying and you will be most amazed at what
you are shown.

Do you remember the man who used to walk up the
hill in Washougal? Do you remember how he would
wave and smile at each passerby. You wondered at
first what this was all about **and why on earth** he was
waving at you. You did not know him and wondered if
he had you confused with someone else. But in time you
came to look forward to his friendly smile and wave. It
aroused a joyful response in your spirit. You have not
seen him for some time now, but you still remember how
you felt when you would see him. You still remember it
was such a wonderful way to start your day. While this
seemed like such a simple thing to do, it is one that had
a very big impact on you. While this action would not
normally be given any special recognition, interesting
on how much you miss it now that it is gone. This then is
an example of true joy**! This is an example of one of
My earth angels who indeed understood the true
meaning of life and his purpose!**

When you respond to that which is your higher
nature, when you are not dictated by the standards of
man then you will be well on your way to understanding your **higher purpose**. Open your hearts then little
ones. Give your burdens to Me. Live in the moment and
you will be well on your way to achieving that which
you are called to do. When you are an open vessel
much will be drawn to you; where there is light, light
will come. Where there then is darkness, darkness will
abound. It is not as though I am stranding you unto an

island by yourself with nothing to assist you. Now you understand all things are possible through Me. When one understands this reality is not a concept they will know this is the reality not the illusion. **There is no place for perception here as I will always get to that which is the heart of the matter.**

I have been talking to you about stories Wendy (the fact that everyone has a story to tell). **While I do not want to minimize any one's story, for each of you is so very important, I want to impress on each of you the story is indeed your own lesson plan. It is what you do with the story that matters. While it may make interesting reading, truthfully, it is the end result which will get the desired response your soul is leading you to. So many of My children do not fully understand this and so they become stalemated. One then need look past the story so they can see the purpose; so they can reach a higher understanding and therefore, be well on the way to achieving their higher purpose.**

Yes, many times one can use a good story. For many their own story prevents them from seeing and understanding what should come as a result. When one dwells on the past, when one is remorseful for that which has already transpired, they indeed waste precious moments in time they cannot recapture.

There will be a judgment day My child. Each of you will be given time to reflect on that which has transpired in your journey. It is therefore imperative you understand all are here to learn, yet it is what you do with the lesson I am most concerned about.

As a human all are enrolled **in the school of life.** There are no exceptions. Each learns according to their own specific needs. Some learn more easily than others and there are those who are more resistant to these lessons. **Whatever the case may be rest assured you are all enrolled and would be wise to understand this is the reality and not the illusion! I want to leave you with this thought today, Wendy, "Our heavenly Father created the world!"**

2/28/2011

"There is much I am sending you now at a very fast pace, Wendy. Know that you are being protected as well as others. You must understand the importance of these writings. I am pleased you are willing to write as the spirit moves you.

There is much being put into place at this time My child. All that I ask of each of you now is to do your part. As you can see **when you are in tune with that which is your gift, that which is your assignment, you will be and are filled with holy enthusiasm.** You will not begrudge yourself of the time involved as you will be most anxious to please the Divine. Your Divine instincts are on full alert now as it is with all of My chosen. I am igniting a spark in each and every one of you. Do not judge one another's part. If it is of good, it is of God. I **will not allow that which I do not want.**

*Do not think about timing now, think only about the immediate and all will come together as planned. This has been and is a part of My master plan for all. You are surprised to read some of what I say, yet you must know this is the truth and it will be the **truth** which overcomes that which is the adversary.*

My children now must understand that which has happened to society as a whole. They must understand the subtleties of Satan and how he has ensconced himself in the lives of all. You are all being given fresh eyes in which to see the world around you and you are being taught the importance of communion with Me at this time. You must increase your ability to discern that which is of Me and to understand this communion is possible.

*Once again PRACTICE, PRACTICE, PRACTICE! Do not look to others for the answers you seek. Come to Me and I will send that which you need. Come to Me and I will show you the way. You must come to Me of your own free will. I allow certain events and circumstances in your life to enable you to understand what is the most important, as well as that which is the priority in each and every one of your lives. Often, this is how I am able to get your attention! Satan would have you think I am an unjust God, yet I use **all situations for good**. You must think as the Divine would have you think. Pray then for right understanding in all things. Learn to think with that which comes from the center of your being, not that which is of the ego. Look to the light in all things, Satan wants and demands you look to the darkness. Trust now you are being guided.*

You are thinking of the word **de-clone.** *You must free your mind in order to write that which I would have you say in this regard. My children today have become a product of society. They have become victims of the adversary held captive by those things which keep one from understanding that which is the very core of their being, that which is the very* **essence** *of your being. Satan has each of his children trapped in the throes of materialism. If you look at the economic conditions in the world today you will see what victims you have all become. There are many of you now who are seeing the effects of this materialism and now are held captive by those things which indeed do not bring lasting happiness. Many now have been thrust into despair and feelings of helplessness.*

While Satan would have you wallow in self pity and indignation I am able to use these circumstances now much to My advantage. For now there are many who understand the true measure of happiness. When you spoke of joy before, there were many, My little one, who did not want to listen. There were many who turned a deaf ear to that which you had to say. **Now you are at a turning point for there are many who are seeking a different way of life.** *There are many of My children who need to understand the importance of these times and what they are capable of through the Divine. They need not fear they do not have what they need to change their lives. It is I who created you and I who provide. My ways are not the ways of man.* **If you but trust there is a higher way you will avail yourself of the gifts which are already there for each** *of you*. *There are more than enough gifts to go around. Satan would have you cling to that which is yours as a catalyst for self, not as a contributing part of the whole. Until My children learn to come together for the betterment of all Satan will indeed keep My kingdom at bay.*

*Years ago I talked to you and Jillian about the art of bartering. There is never a better time than present to put this into practice. You could in fact even try this at an art show. That is for later. My people do not need to lack for anything. You must understand each of your gifts does have a value to others. If one could think on this concept, practice this concept, promote this concept, the results would be astonishing for all involved. For discussion purposes think of your gift as a trade (skill). Now I want you to think in terms of trade as to exchange. When you accept one indeed is responsible for one another this then makes a great deal of sense and frees one **from consumerism as it is practiced today.**"*

3/1/2011

"My little one, you were worried your enthusiasm for the painting class would get in the way of your writing. You see now such is not the case when you are working in My will. You will come to see all things are now working for the greater good. I was most anxious for you to attend your first class and am now giving you pieces which in the end will delight you as they all come together!

*You wonder why I do not tell you all ahead of time. That is because I want the two of you to **stay in the moment** and you will not miss a beat! When I say beat, I am thinking of your hearts. Allow your hearts then to swell and you indeed will understand much as the week's progress.*

*You are being led now and will see the fruits of your faithfulness. I am showing you how I plant the seed in My children. When My children live in the moment they are able to follow up on this seed. As earth angels you must learn to plant seeds for others. **You must teach My earth angels how to recognize the seeds I plant and they will not miss that which they are being led to.***

Others will see the joy which I am increasing in each of you and they will wonder once again at the transformation. This joy is contagious and will have an impact on those you are in contact with. I will bring new people into your lives now and you must trust there is indeed something to glean from each and everyone in your path.

*You will be filled with a renewed compassion for that which you are called to do. **You will see how by tapping into this energy they will be filled with holy enthusiasm**! For many of My children, due to the **rigors** of life, have been trapped in a world which does not nurture that which comes naturally. **When one then becomes free and open to this energy flow the spirit can once again be heard**.*

When a child is young they are so receptive to the creative energy which comes from within. It is so important as a child develops this creative energy is not harnessed. This creative energy must be allowed to flow.

You find it interesting I used the word rigor. When you do not fully understand the meaning of the word do not change it, simply look up the meaning. Rigor means discipline. What then does the word discipline imply? How does one feel when they are disciplined, **or should I say living in a life dominated by discipline?** *Yes, My daughter you are most amazed at the how discipline is defined. Think then on these words: control, restraint, authority, punishment, chastise, correct,* **self-control, restraint, strictness!** *These words apply to so many of My children and the world's they have created for themselves. What they need to understand is how they have allowed themselves to live their lives as victims of society. They are held captive then by the standards mankind has set. These standards are set by the ego, not by that which is of the Divine.*

When one then releases their creative energy it opens the spirit to the promise of a more fulfilling way of life, a life that is not full of rigors and restraints. It allows one to see possibilities they truly had not allowed themselves to explore before. *Are you understanding, My daughter?*

You are thinking of your writing. I want you to see the possibilities as you open the creative side of your being. As you allow yourself to understand that which you are capable of. Wendy, you and Jillian have always worked for me. There is much you will come to understand.

You understand much now as you write and you must not worry so about what you are going to write. For when you say the Divinity Prayer each of you is being given Divine inspiration. I want you to look at others now as a mirror, a reflection of yourself. In some cases this will be a very eye opening experience. It will show you those aspirations within yourself you need to refine. **Yes, refine means to purify**.

Make sure then My little ones your aspirations are of the Divine and not of the ego. This is a way to keep the adversary from filling you up with your own self importance. You all are given gifts and must be careful not to be puffed up in these gifts. **There is a difference between enthusiasm and self-importance. When one is filled with holy enthusiasm they must always give credit to the Divine!**

When one proceeds knowing they are in the will of our heavenly Father they have faith these gifts indeed will be an inspiration to all. Remember what is freely given must be given in this mind set (attitude). You are listening now Wendy, as you write. There will be time for you to reflect after you are done. When one is completing the task at hand it is best to reflect after the fact, as this reflection takes one away from the moment. You must therefore trust you are writing the words which are of the Divine. This is an exercise then of faith as well for My children. Each of you must trust you are being inspired by the Divine. Many times My works are stalemated because of doubt. **Do not be Doubting Thomas' now! When you do something My little ones do it for Me.** Use all that you do for the betterment of others. Use your creative energy as a beacon of light for others.

Do not be messengers of darkness. My earth angels now must be messengers of light. **Take the importance off of self and place the importance on that which is the essence of life**. Lift one another up to Me and watch as My work prevails. There are many in the heavens who indeed are watching you now My child. There are many in the heavens who are smiling at the two of you. They are filled with glee. I must say there were some who were becoming increasingly alarmed! They too have a challenge with Divine timing. Even they tend to become impatient at times. You are smiling now My little ones. I know this is the part of the writing you enjoy My daughter. Picture then in your mind My daughter those in the heavens who are applauding the two of you now. You both are so very loved.

Think on those who have gone and prepared the way before you. They are so pleased at what is transpiring now. Smile, for there is much which is taking place at this time for all of My earth angels! Remember when we talked about the **Great Plan**? Think now on Dorothy Day. You have not thought about her for some time. Reflect then on when her works were stalemated for awhile. Think then on what the message was there. She needed to appreciate the gifts of others and understand how important it is for **all to come together in** *likeness and humility.* *This is why so many under-takings fail My daughter. It is not that they do not start with good intentions.* **They fail or run into obstacles because of the ego, because one loses sight of Divine inspiration.** *It is because often man tries to take control rather than trusting all will be taken care of.* **Always then think on that which is of purity. Are one's intentions pure and if so what is the motivation behind one's intentions? This is a good way to make certain one's intentions are in line with that which is of the Divine.** *When you are feeling uncertain simply come to Me and I will show you the right way."*

3/2/2011

"A creative mind opens the mind to new possi-bilities. It opens up the senses and acts as a con-duit for the Divine. When this energy is allowed to flow it limits one's dependency on the mind. In a sense then it opens one's instinctive (natural) abilities or most specifically inherent abilities.

When one exercises their inherent abilities they are filled with a natural energy which feeds the soul and not the mind. When the soul is satisfied one will then experience a more holistic form of life, the life which has always been available to all. When this creative energy is released it forms a barrier from those negative thoughts of the mind which create internal dis-ease.

Yes, I talked to you much during the night My little one, I enjoyed your creativity! It was fun watching you as you clicked the light on and off on your cell phone so that you might see what you were writing! It is as Jillian said, "You will not forget, Wendy." I am so enjoying this process with you!

*You now are starting to understand why I used the word clone or de-clone in the process of converting one from mind practices to that of **soulful practices**. You are all individuals and unique. Yet, your minds have become so cluttered with the rigors of life you are not able to appreciate and share that which is the most special part of each and every one of you. I have talked to you about many things and there is much more to come.*

*It is easy to see how **inhibited** man has become. Man in his quest to achieve has shut off that which comes naturally from within. In doing so he has buried his intuitive sense (inhibition **resists intuition**). So much so when he does experience flashes of intuition he disregards these feelings, and as a result does not respond to that which the soul is guiding him towards. There are so many of My children now who become self conscious when asked to share their talents. That is because many do not think their talent holds value in the world today. Nothing could be farther from the truth. For I tell you it is the culmination of these gifts which indeed will change the course of the world. One need then bare their soul for all to see! By sharing the deepest and most precious part of each of you the world will indeed be experiencing a soulful and more meaningful way of life.*

One must heighten their senses. *When you learn to live in the moment each and every sense must*

be paid attention to. Do you remember the first time
you smelled a pot of coffee brewing, the first time you
as a child delighted in the floral scents which perme-
ate the spring air? The expression **take time to smell
the roses** is an exercise in appreciating the senses.
It is the same then with listening, truly listening. It is
the same with taste and of course the ability to see the
world through the eyes of the Divine. In sharpening
one's senses one is able to slow down the clanging of the
mind. One is able to open the door to a more soulful way
of life. Yes, you are correct I am taking all of you back
to that which you intrinsically experienced as a child.
I am stripping you now of many practices which have
kept you trapped in an unfulfilling and meaningless way
of life!

As your Father in heaven I want to take care of your
needs. As your Father in heaven I know that which
is of your heart's desire. Yet, as any conscientious
Father would do, there are times your wants will not
be attended to. In fact, as you know I will sometimes
close those doors which are not in your soul's best interest. For in closing the door lies an opportunity for your
soul to open up.

Mankind refers to the right and left side of the brain.
By linking man's responses and abilities in this manner
no thought then is given to the most important aspect
of one's being. This implies all thoughts, feelings and
actions are indeed a product of one's mind. **Nothing is
farther from the truth! When you eliminate that
which is of a compulsive nature you are able**

to avail yourself of all of your senses. You have
a heightened awareness of all aspects of your being.
This heightened awareness of the senses feeds the soul.
When My children behave in a compulsive manner they
stifle their creative ability. This then stifles their growth
and ultimately one's ability to serve. Man's quest for
knowledge has indeed distanced him from that which
is of the Divine. It has indeed created a **barrier to the
senses, to one's soul** that is deeply imbedded in the
world today.

I want you to think on Michaelangelo for a moment.
I chose him because of the holy work he did for Me. He
could not have painted that which he is so known for
had he not opened the channels for his creative energy to
flow. This was not then energy of the mind. This indeed
was an example of using one's natural gifts and talents
for the benefit of others. Although in the beginning it was
used for the religious, it still remains as an inspiration
for all walks of life to appreciate. This then is a perfect
example of that which is possible for all. This then is
Divine inspiration not mind inspiration. Do not then
allow inhibitions to block your intuitions; that which
comes from the deepest part of you. Do not allow these
inhibitions, (a product of one's ego) to deprive you and
others of your own abilities through Me.

Many times I have used the terminology **go to the
cave within**. There are those who talk a great deal
about meditation or more appropriate the practice of
meditation. This is a practice man uses to encourage
one's contemplative nature. When I refer to the cave

within I want you to avail yourself of this safe haven which resides in each and every one of My children. It is in this haven you will connect with your soul. When you then go to the cave within you leave behind that which is of this world and now are in that which is of the Divine.

This is your sanctuary. This sanctuary is not tainted by the adversary yet can be blocked by that which is of this world. It is there for each and every one of My children. Yet, many do not know how to avail themselves of this most sacred part of their being. While the practice of meditation assists one in settling the mind it for many discourages communion with Me. Although this was not the original intent, the idea of participating in the practice of meditation deters many of My children.

One does not have to meditate to avail themselves of this most sacred part of one's being. One does not have to be a guru; one does not have to be a counselor. One only needs to understand you all have been created in this manner.

If you look up the word meditate you will see it means to; engage in contemplation or reflection. For many, meditation then intercedes with this process. You do not need that which is of an external nature to avail yourself of your sanctuary. This is where you indeed are able to commune with the Divine. This is not a practice in one way conversation. This is where you are able to converse with your heavenly Father knowing that which you hear is of Him. When you go to the cave within you can be assured you will indeed understand the true meaning of life and your own purpose. As it is with any relationship the more time you spend with the Divine the deeper the relationship will become. You will **trust** this relationship as you trust the relationships of those closest to your heart. I am the only Being you have at your disposal twenty four hours a day. No matter where you are, no matter what time of day it is, you can avail yourself of this sanctuary **(a safe harbor which you can retreat to at any given moment).**

Do you think I as your heavenly Father would have created you any other way? Do you think I would have left you without a means and a way to actively commune with Me? What kind of a Father do you think I would be if I did not provide you with this sanctuary? I am there to protect and guide My children. Mankind

in his quest to find Me has succeeded in closing the
door to that which manifests in all who desire to avail
themselves of the cave within, this safe harbor! This has
always been there for all. As it was in the day of Adam
and Eve it is there for all who choose to open themselves
to that which is of the Divine (to that which is of the
Father's will).

*I am saying this to you little one as simply as
I can*. You must only write the words I am asking you
to write. Man complicates far too many things. When
there is confusion and chaos this is not of the Divine.
For I want My children to understand that which is of
Me. Why would I try to complicate that which will assist
them in their journey? You are all capable of a much
richer and more fulfilling way of life than you have
experienced before. I will teach you, if you will but listen
to that which I am revealing at this time.

All it takes then is a willingness to relearn that which
you have been taught of the world. Now My little one
take the time to learn that which is of your Father's
world. For I and I alone **created** this world and indeed
this took much creativity of that you can be certain.
I have left nothing out. I have left nothing to chance. It
is up to each and every one of My children to decide.
*One can either continue to live by the standards
of man or avail yourself to that which is of the
Divine*. I will send those to you who will assist you in
this new way of life. I will send those to you with like
minds. I will send those to you who understand the
importance of nurturing one's soul. *This desire for*

each will manifest into a new way of life for those who choose to avail themselves. You must teach others Wendy of this. You must not ever set yourselves above those who do not yet understand. Yet, you simply must be willing to share that which you know to be true. You and Jillian must help others to understand what is the reality for all! You must help them to see the possibilities through the Divine. These are exciting times for all. When you start and end your day with that which is of Me I will bring to you that which you need. Live in the moment.

Have you noticed how many of My children seem to be rushing from one thing to another? Even in yourself you have seen how you need to keep from concerning yourself with the next moment. Simply enjoy that which is of the moment and there will be time for all."

3/4/2011

"You are beginning to see bits and parts of the Great Plan My daughter. The plan made reference to years ago. You are starting to see how this can all come together and most important how it will come to fruition. When this plan becomes initiated you will begin to see the battle begin. For those who are listening, those who partake indeed will be My soldiers on earth.

You as My earth angels, My messengers of light, will understand the part you play. You are seeing now it is my timing that is taking place. You are starting to understand the **bigger picture for all.** That is why you cannot afford to cover one another's gifts! You must

simply do the part you know you are called to do and all
will be well. All then will succeed as in My plan.

You doubted this day would come My little ones. You
were so afraid that you had missed the boat. Yet, see
how well you listened when the spirit moved you. I have
told you before there are many in the heavens who are
watching over My earth angels now. They are ready to
make the necessary moves whenever called to keep all of
you on track. For this reason it is crucial all of you spend
time with Me on a daily basis. You do not look to man
for the answers you seek. For the answers you seek now
lie within the confines of the Divine. These are holy times
for holy messengers.

Do not question your worth or your validity.
There is no room for doubt in the days ahead as I will
give each of you all that you need to succeed in your
earthly endeavors. When you are filled with an energy
and enthusiasm to continue listen to that which comes
from within. I will give you that which you need to continue and I will stop you when it is time. You are so filled
with the spirit, and this is a sign you are indeed working
in My will, My daughter, **for I am taking other daily
activities and desires away at this time.** This is the
way it will be with all of My earth angels in the days and
weeks ahead.

When an idea comes to you seemingly out of the blue
I encourage you, I implore you to follow up on the idea.
If it is of God, then it is good. **It is not that I want you
and Jillian to be in charge of these ideas, simply**

be seed planters and watch others cultivate that which is to be done. They will willingly take on that which they are called to do, that which they are passionate about. In other words they will be the best man for the job!(smile); the best earth angel for the job!

When you then respond to that which you are enthusiastic about you are filled with joy as are those around you. For you all are fulfilling your Divine purpose. No task is too small as it is when all the parts come together. When man can work in harmony with one another the **greater good will prevail. Do not be afraid to exercise your higher self!**

There is much I wish to speak to you about today. There is much I spoke of throughout the night. You will find this often will be the case on those days you are not able to write. Are you still surprised just when you think there is nothing more to write about more comes? I will let you know when it is time My little ones. You will not have to force it, the same as you will not have to decide what to write and not what to write.

You and Jillian now are refining, relearning those things which I have taught you. What you learn now will be of benefit to many and can be used if you obey that which I say. I love you both very much. I love all of My children very much. As earth angels you must understand the love I have for all of My children. I have talked to you about the **"dark night of the soul."** *You are wondering about some of the internal feelings you have towards some people. There are those you come* in contact with and will come in contact with who live in darkness. Their souls are crying out in anguish. It is not that these people are not good people in many ways. These are people who for one reason or another have blocked themselves from a relationship with the Divine. These individuals do not take responsibility for their own life choices and as a result often misunderstand the true meaning and purpose of life. They look then to the mind for the answers they seek. This will never be where they will find what their souls are so desperately crying out for.

As an earth angel you can sense those who do not cultivate a relationship with the Divine. Be not afraid of the feelings this will provoke in you, rather look to Me for that which you need to understand regarding these individuals who cross your path. **When you feel as though you cannot make a difference in their lives nothing can be farther from the truth**. Do not then let fear keep you from this relationship. You must remember your actions, many times, will speak a great deal louder than words. **Words are empty My little one if the actions do not follow!**

When you are in the will of the Divine My little one you will not get distracted. Rather, you will find a great deal of dis-ease when you do not listen to that which you are called to do for Me. Your desires are of the Father when you are working in My regard.

When you see or hear something which stays with you now there is indeed a holy reason for what I am bringing to you. You are thinking about the man who had a heart attack and was kept alive by more than twenty individuals who took turns doing CPR on him. There were many still standing in line when the medics finally arrived. What does this then tell you about the basic nature of man or better yet, what do you truly think this message is about for My earth angels?

Man is intrinsically good, yet there are many who have lost touch with those basic feelings, those basic feelings which allow one to fully experience the richness of life. For there is a longing to help one another, yet the world has become so chaotic many do not understand the secret to living. **The secret to living is in the giving.** It is only through one's life journey many hearts become hardened and many turn a deaf ear. These are the little souls who are so hungry for their Father. They are longing for the comfort only He can give. **These souls do not understand unconditional love as they always put conditions on the love they give.** This is not how to come to know the true essence of joy, the true meaning of life. Yet, one cannot understand that which they will not accept. There are many of My children who indeed do good works and they still are not satisfied. They are not at peace and often become embittered as they cannot find what they are searching and longing for. The more they do the less at peace they become. For what they seek will never come from the external. **The peace they seek will never come from people, places or things.**

I want to talk to you about **creative energy** now and I want both of you to listen very carefully. Yes, this is what you were trying to understand for much of the night. When one exercises their creative energy they must be careful they use this energy as a conduit of the soul. **When one exercises the creative side of one's being this then is a way to <u>release inhibitions</u> which are a barrier to the soul.** Many of My children are creative, yet often this profound fact escapes them.

In working for the Father one must understand the true nature of their gifts and talents and exercise them accordingly. This is not to take away from expression, it is simply to help one understand that which they have been given to accomplish the will of the Divine.

I want to talk about the five senses now so one will understand these are part and parcel of the body, the temporal body. These senses are a part of the human condition. **There is indeed another part of the human condition, the only part which is not temporal**. It is the part of you which lives on forever and ever and ever. There are those who label this part as a sixth sense. These individuals are often said to have psychic abilities. Many say this sixth sense is not connected to religion; it is not connected to the Divine. While this sense is not afforded only to the religious it is available to all. **Man would like one to think the way to develop this sixth sense is through the mind. Nothing is farther from the truth**. This is ones internal sense, this is what you come into the world with and this is what you leave with. What man does not understand is how you activate this sense. **When man**

understands this ability is of the Divine, that it is not temporal, He will understand the importance of communion with Me. *For it is through this communion you will come to know that which is the reality, not that which is the illusion. Many do not seek this relationship because Satan would have one think they are not capable of a richer and fuller way of life.* **I give you this example of the sixth sense as man has understood it to be so you will have the tools you need to help others understand the workings of the cave within.**

Many times these subjects seem deep for you, Wendy, as you write them, yet to others these words will act as a catalyst to that which is keeping them from accomplishing their assignments. I can leave nothing to chance now My child and so as you see and hear things you must write about them. For when they stay with you they have a purpose, a holy purpose. Do not become frustrated when there are those who do not understand that which you are called to do. It is not of their concern as you should not concern yourselves with their opinion. **Remember who you work for and why you work for Me. Remember from whence you come and all will be well for each of you.**

I talked about fatalism early on and want you to understand you must guard yourselves now against those thoughts which rob you of your joy. If all were indeed futile you would not be called to act in these days. As before, I caution you to not react to that which you cannot control. It is so much better then to respond to that which is of the Divine. For you are being given Divine Inspiration!

You will not need to look for the signs you need only be open to the signs as they will be coming at a rapid rate now. Avoid that which is perception and look to the truth, the heart of the matter. *As earth angels you will experience many feelings now at a heightened level. You once again are in the process of purification and must accept these feelings as such. Do not spend time belaboring these feelings as before. Rather, pay attention to these feelings as they are giving you a message. Often when you feel at dis-ease it is because you are being given a new understanding of yourself or someone else. When this occurs simply say the Divinity Prayer and all will be well.* ***You must not be frightened for your tool against the adversary is my unconditional love for you****. When you walk with Me you will be able to practice unconditional love freely. Your ways now must **not** be the ways of the world, but rather the ways of My world. This is not as before when you were learning the art of a joy-filled life. The time now has come to put all of the pieces together.*

Although you know more than many never act as though you know more than many. *While you need not be humble in My regard you must be an open vessel for others in order to implement your teachings. In this way you will attract those who otherwise would not avail themselves to you. There are still far too many who confuse that which is of the Divine with that of religion."*

3/8/2011

Although it has only been since yesterday it seems like forever since I have written as I am used to spending time with you now in the morning. When I am not able to do so I feel empty somehow. I have a new IPad now and hope this will aid in the writing of the book and those thoughts which are now coming at a very fast pace. I know now when I hear that which you are sharing with me and I know those thoughts which are keeping me in a quandary.

There is so much happening in the world now at such a fast and alarming pace it is difficult to really know for certain that which You would have included in the book and that which You would have me save for a later date. I feel so strongly now events are going to keep on happening which indeed are the precursor for the final battle between good and evil.

I am rather lethargic today and am wondering truly what the reason is? You have shared so much in the past two weeks. I pray I will do that well which You are calling me to do.

"My daughter you must understand you cannot fail. For I see the desire and enthusiasm you and Jillian have for the task at hand. You are correct there is much happening in the world at this time. Yet, you and My chosen need not be alarmed for I tell you in the final battle good will triumph over evil. You must not allow yourself or other earth angels to become discouraged. Discouragement as you know is not of the Divine. I will

give you all of the necessary tools each of you needs to complete your earthly assignment. I want all of you now to focus on that which is of the Divine. I want you to think on those things you can do to keep yourself sheltered in your own sanctuary. It is here you will find the comfort and solace you need as time goes on. You must not look at that which is happening in the world as a negative. I know it hurts you to see the ways in which Satan has managed to rear his ugly head in so many areas, yet you must not let this keep you from your mission. For I have given all of you the tools you need to awaken many from their complacent behavior. In reading the **Earth Angel book** questions will be answered for those who have been longing to fulfill their purpose.

All of you now will understand how My kingdom shall be brought to this earth. It is My chosen people who understand what it will take to bring My kingdom to reality. All of you now must look to the light. You must be responsible for one another and you must share that with each other that you know to be true. You will see increasing signs as time passes. These signs will confirm the world as you know it today indeed is changing. You must not listen to those who do not **know Me and you must trust that which you hear in the night. You cannot hear, you will not understand if you do not go to the cave within.**

I have told you how to commune with Me. I have shown you how you must now allow your creative energy to flow. You must live in the moment. Do not harbor remorse for the past and most of all do not dwell on future events. This will not serve any purpose towards that which each of you is to accomplish. You must pay attention to all that is around you. You must be on high alert at all times and you will not miss those signs and messages I am bringing to each of My chosen children. Every time you connect with another human being now you must share that which you know to be truth. Do not become harbors of darkness rather always be a beacon of light for those you come in contact with. For it is in the light one can clearly see. What is the reality? What is the heart of the matter?

Satan will try to **implode** you with negative energy. You must keep your guard up then for the tactics the adversary will now use on each of you. When it seems as though nothing is happening or that you might be off track from that which is your purpose, simply come to Me and I will help you in your heavenly endeavors.

There are so many in the heavens who are watching over you now. They are watching as never before, for they too understand the tools and means Satan has in his arsenal at this time. The good news is Satan cannot know of what we speak. He cannot know what takes place in each of your sanctuaries. You must be careful now who you address your concerns to. Also remember often **the answer lies in the asking of the question**! If you are not certain of what the Divine is showing you than you need to ask for some sign of confirmation. For I will give you the confirmation you need when it is of Me. This is part of the covenant I have formed with My children. I will not leave my soldiers floundering in these times.

Your guardians are by your side now every moment of every day. They love it so when you acknowledge their presence. They have been watching you as you have moved towards this part of your journey. To say things are at a feverish pitch in the heavens is to put it mildly. St. Michael has his entire legion on alert now and many already are engaged in battle.

Soon each of you will be actively engaged in battle as well. Say the Divinity prayer on a daily basis and you can move forward knowing you are filled with the Holy Spirit. You cannot imagine the depth of My love for each and every one of you. Yet, I tell you when you respond to that which is of the Divine you will be **positively** infused with energy in the days and weeks ahead. I will fill each of you with holy **enthusiasm.** You will experience the highest form of **altruism** as you share your gifts freely with one another. When you ask for your Father's will you indeed will be filled with the **compassion** which comes of Divine understanding.

> **P- Positive**
> **E-Enthusiasm**
> **A-Altruistic**
> **C- Compassion**
> **E-Enlightened**

Know then My little ones you now will be filled with the **peace which surpasses human understanding**. You are now fully enlightened children in God's *army. I and My legion will provide a fortress around you. Your souls now are one with the Divine. You must remember your bodies are merely temporal, only a means in which to house your soul while you accomplish that which is your higher purpose. Feed your soul now as you feed your body.*

Share the good news with those you come in contact with. You all will know when to speak and when to remain silent. When it is of Me the words will flow easily and seemingly with little effort. When it is not of Me you will sense the difference. I have great faith in your abilities My little ones, if that were not the case I would have chosen another for the job you are about to do. No task is too small; no gift shall remain unused in the coming together of My kingdom on earth. These harmonious works will be for the betterment of all mankind. The ego will once and for all be abated as greed will no longer prevail."

Wendy was so anxious to share that which Jesus had asked her to write she was bursting at the seams to finish that which He would have her share. Yet, she knew when He had shared all that He wanted in the book she would know it was time to stop writing and start compiling.

For this reason she was certain each and every person would know when to act on their gifts. She knew all gifts would come together now in Divine timing and she need only respond to that which was her part. All His children need do was simply respond to the promptings of their soul and go to the cave within and they would indeed know their true purpose and from whence they came. Their soul has known this all along; that which is the reality and that which is of the Divine!

3/11/2011

"You are listening now My little one and beginning to truly understand the message and purpose of the book. All you need do is write that which I tell you and all will be on the pages as I desire.

***This book is to be a guide and inspiration for many**. Think of it as a tool which will help others understand that which is of the Divine. As I have told you I want all of My children to pay attention to the times in which they live. They can only do this little one by living in the moment.*

*For that reason I want My children to focus only on the immediate events at hand and not become distracted by that which has happened either in the past or that which they think will happen in the future. For no man can truly foretell that which is to come or the exact timing of what is to come. Remember, if you will, heavenly time is not the same as on earth. When one goes to the cave within they will get the answers they seek. This is there, as I have said, for all My children to partake of. **Do not spend time now with those who do not desire to hear My voice. Do not spend time debating with others what is or is not to come. This will serve no purpose and simply prove as another huge distraction.***

There then can be no distractions now! Please, all of My children, take heed to what I say and listen to what the spirit is calling you to do. You all are equipped with the gifts and talents you need to do your part. All I ask now is you listen and simply do that which is required of each of you.

If you could but imagine the magnitude of love I have for each and every one of you then you would understand that which I say now is the reality. This has been the reality for all since the beginning of time. When you feel as though another person does not quite get it, then you must understand it is because they are not listening. Trust Me when I say all of My children have and will be given every chance to know what the true meaning of life is and what their mission is here on this earth.

All of you are living in very special times. *As now you will see the world change right before your eyes. You will see that mankind indeed has a much higher capacity than experienced in the world so far. Your job then is to help others understand the importance of these times and assure them of the covenant I have formed with My people. Do you remember when I said if there were no books, if there were no churches, if there was no information on hand, as the current world knows it to be, My children will get the answers to that which they seek directly from Me.*

There is still so much I want to share with My children if you can just be patient and not get distracted this process will go even more quickly than before. Do not get distracted or think ahead little one, just simply be in the here and now. I will give you the words and fill you with holy enthusiasm. My children then must trust all will be filled with holy enthusiasm in these times!

I want to talk about free will for a moment so you can understand that which you are dealing with and that which you have been responding to. You must understand in order to shift to that of the Divine you must have faith and know from whence each of you comes. When you close yourself off to this connection you close yourself off to that which is part and parcel of your soul.

Some may choose to ignore that which is of the Divine. As your Father in heaven I am now asking you to trust Me. I am pleading with all of you to listen and spend time in communion with Me. My ways, as you will soon find out, are indeed not the ways of man, not the ways of the world. Yet, if you but trust Me I will help those who believe to establish My kingdom on earth.

When another opposes that which you know to be true and they will not support what I have asked each of you to do, this is when you must shake the dust from your feet and move on. You cannot impose your will on another the same as I will not impose My will on any of My children. I do not go where I am not received. I am always available but cannot be heard if I am not acknowledged. So then you must understand, if someone will not acknowledge Me they will not acknowledge that which is of Me.

You think about transgressions, those sins of the family which are passed down generation to generation. You must not spend time lamenting over choices you made as a result of these transgressions. Simply understand that which is the heart of the matter. I asked my Father to forgive all for I knew the level of transgressions that would transcend throughout generations. What is most important in the end is you learn from those choices and do good works now in the name of our Father.

It is very important My children are balanced in all areas of their lives in the days ahead. You must be physically strong as well as nurture your souls more now than ever before. Listen to the still voices inside of you and you will be led to those of like spirit and minds. Do not think then anything now is of coincidence.

Do not put off until tomorrow what I need you to do today. You must remember I and the angels above are guiding all of you at this time. When you are confused about something or it seems as though you are getting conflicting information you must come to Me and I will show you that which is the truth. You will know those who are of Me and those who are not of Me. Do not waste energy on those things you cannot control. Spend your time doing that which you can accomplish through Me. Use those gifts which I have equipped each of you with.

I have talked about creative energy. This is so important as it acts as a barrier to that which is of the mind. More important it shuts down the thoughts which are not of the Divine. By opening your creative side then you are able to express that which is of your higher nature, that which comes from the very center of your being.

It is difficult for My children to understand there are those who will consciously reject these truths. They respond to the ego and will not allow that which is of the spirit to penetrate their being. They strive to achieve only that which is of the material plain and many will do so at the expense of another's well being. It is prudent you understand this fact as these are the people who are entrapped in the snares of Satan and his legion. These are the people in the end you will have cause to turn away from. I hope and pray many will see the error of their ways, yet there will be those who will not accept the true reality.

3/12/2011 to 3/15/2011

"My daughter today I want to talk to you about fear. This is very important for My people to understand in the days and weeks ahead. Fear is not of the Father, it is one of the primary tools of the adversary and now he will use it well as events begin to unfold. For this reason I ask My children to limit their exposure to the media. Although I want all of you to be in the moment and pay attention you must not focus on that which you can- not control. As in the earth quake of Japan you must not listen now to those reports that may or may not be accurate. This keeps one's mind in a state of turmoil which then prohibits your ability to settle down and commune with Me.

When one is plagued with fear it renders one immo- bile. Please listen to this and understand there are many things now which are out of your control. This is where your faith must be very active and very strong. Do not

then utter words of fear or spread that which is a catalyst for Satan and his adversary. Fear promotes fear!
Fear never promotes mindful actions or activities. When
you therefore come to Me, I will tell you that which you
all need to know at the appropriate time. Do not look to
the media, to the politicians for any answers you need at
this time.

When you cannot hear that which I am saying then
you need to trust I am all knowing. Spend each and
every day with Me. **Go to your sanctuary within
and stay with Me until a conversation does
indeed manifest!** For some of you this may be at
different times throughout the day. It may not be the
same for everyone.

I am asking all of My children to keep a journal
now. Simply write that which is of concern or anything
which is on your heart. By keeping a journal you will
bear witness to the answers which I am giving you in
communion. This will give you the reassurance you need
as time passes.

There will be those of you now who are actively
seeking a church home. I tell you this when you worship
keep your eyes on Me and that which you know to be
true. If words are spoken now which do not support
the truths I have shared with you then you will not find
solace or comfort there.

Wendy be not anxious as to what you write, I will
give you the words that I want My people to hear in
these days. Sometimes I want My children to reflect on

that which I have written so that you might see firsthand the importance of what you write.

You must refresh all people's minds of that which are the tools Satan will use in the weeks and months ahead. Many of your hearts are aching at this time regarding the events in Japan. I am watching all of My children now to see how they respond to these events. Many prayer requests have been sent my way and I hear them all. Yet, there are so many My little ones who turn a deaf ear. I look then at the measure of each of your hearts in these days as this could be anyone now who is laden with these types of natural events. You must understand no one is exempt from that which is of the creator. This is a huge wake up call for mankind. Do you not find it interesting how quickly the media has shifted from the urgency of Libya to the urgency in Japan? Why do you think that is? The answers you seek lie in the confines of each of your sanctuaries. When My children come to Me they will find many answers to that which is now manifesting in these times.

You are correct My daughter there is much to come. There is much that no man can foresee coming in the near future. These nuclear threats will indeed become very real in the near future. This is not of God! This is of man and should give you a good indication of what mankind has brought into this world as you and My children know it today. Therefore, look to the heart of man and look to those who exemplify compassion and are forthright about what they know to be true.

Now you are truly understanding about the sharing of gifts and talents, Wendy. Cast your eyes on the heavens above and do that which brings you and those you love closer to Me. Share that which you know to be true and set an example for those who are around you. There is naught to fear for those who know Me My child. Yet, there is much evil running rampant in this world today and the battle will be great. There will be many who do not come to Me in time and as a result they will suffer much throughout eternity. Try now not to focus on that which is the physical, rather, focus on that which is of the Divine. I want all of My children to take care of their bodies to strengthen them for the days ahead. Your bodies are but temporal and it is your souls now which truly need the most attention.

Remember it is always darkest before the dawn and that is what will transpire in grave proportions now before My kingdom reigns on this earth. The safety My children will seek comes from the cave within where they will be guided now just as if I was walking in front of them. Please Wendy, let My people understand this most important truth. For when all around you is taken away this is where they will find their comfort, solace and as said before much needed guidance. I will not fail you, I implore you then to respond to My call and write all that I tell you to write in these times. This must now be the priority.

I am not asking you to be a prophet little one, I am asking you to teach others about this holy sanctuary. For this is how we will fight the adversary. This is a place he cannot enter and he cannot know that which I tell my children in these days. Satan will use fear, world events, greed, and depression, all of the negative emotions now to keep you from coming to Me. His primary goal is to prevent My children from hearing that which is the real-ity, from hearing that which is the truth.

Saint Michael and his legion now are on high alert. There will be many who try to capitalize on these anx-ious times. Yet, when all come together in the name of the Father you will have the strength and the tools you need to bring My kingdom to earth.

Do not let the little children become frightened, Wendy. I will protect them, I will insulate them. I know how you love them so as I love the little children. Simply

make sure you have on hand those things they will
need in the physical plain to keep them safe and secure.
I will warn you of future events as I have told you now
regarding your government. Do not trust the political
arena now. Rely on your own knowledge and rely on
that which comes from the interior.

**I want you to title the book "Earth Angels".
You are My messengers of light in the world
today. My earth angels will lead all out of
the darkness into the light. They will find this
light in their holy sanctuaries within. This will
be the strongest message you can give them.
Show them the steps. Review the steps that I
have given you and make them abundantly
clear for those who read the book. You will
see the magnitude of these teachings; you will
see the importance of these writings for all of
My people. Do not worry about what mankind
thinks of these writings. You and Jillian have
seen Me, you know the truth. I have shown you
the truth over the years so you would be ready
for these times. Satan will attack you through
that which is of the illusion, yet you must stand
steadfast. You must write exactly as I have told
you to write. I will shelter the two of you and
send you those you need to get this done. Thank
you for responding to My call little ones, for
I need all of My earth angels to act now. There is
no time to waste.**

3/16/2011

"I have come to you in the night. Know this, when you wake up with a thought which is very clear this is to be written. Many times My little one you are so very cautious what you hear is of Me and not that of the adversary. Do not worry as what you write now will be verified. Remember, the adversary cannot know what you hear in communion with Me.

Fear renders one immobile, yet I am telling all of My children now to pay attention to that which they hear from Me. There is much happening behind the scenes and now you must only rely on that which comes from the interior.

I have told you things are not as they seem in many situations and now you must pay attention to your holy intuition. I spoke of a holocaust in Japan and you are confused? Yes, it means many people killed and the dictionary refers to holocaust as a nuclear disaster. One now cannot believe what they are hearing regarding the containment of this radiation. They have created a monster and now this monster will be unleashed throughout the world.

Wendy, you are not comfortable with this but you need to believe now in that which you write and I need you to share with others how important it is they come to Me for the answers they seek. They must learn to trust in what they hear in communion with Me. Yes, they have found traces of the radiation in the water. There are drops that can be put in the water to counteract water which has been contaminated. You will find that which you need.

Much of what is being written now can be gleaned and you will see how some of these writings will fit into the book. Events which happen will verify what has already been written. When you look at what the people of Japan are concerned about you will see it is not Mother Nature now they are most terrified of. What they are now most concerned about is indeed man made. This is an example of mankind's futile attempt to control that which should never have been created in the first place.

Do you see a pattern here now? This is a prime example of a select few who now have been able to put the lives of millions in jeopardy. Do you then wonder at the level of trust man has had for one another or would you simply call it complacency. So many innocent victims are affected by the decisions of a few!

*You need to understand then how important it is for all My children to come to Me. It is difficult for your government to wrap its arms around the myriad of problems as they are now occurring at a rapid rate. This also is part of Satan's arsenal; he is now using the tools of **distraction and confusion.** Do you see the importance in the statement "you all have a responsibility to one another?" Everything Wendy is intertwined. **Every action creates another action**. If then it is not a right action then right action will not follow. If it is a wrong action then wrong action will follow. I want you and Jillian to think on this as wrong action always affects others. This* is a different way to talk about negative versus positive. We are talking about how one's actions affect another. You will now see how other's actions have indeed effected the world and are accountable for the state of the world as you are now witnessing.

I have taught you to focus on the solution and not the problem. This is what I want all of My children to focus on now. Satan is using the media to keep one from focusing on that which is the solution. You all must come together in the days ahead to create a better world for all. Each person then must do their part to change the course of the tide. What has already happened cannot be undone and as a result many will suffer. Can you not see the injustice in this? Yet, I tell you now to act in the days and weeks ahead. Simply do those things each of you is being asked to do.

When one actively seeks to change their life style they will be able to respond to that which comes from within. Please encourage My children to slow down and listen to that which is coming from the interior. For this dis-ease they are experiencing is a warning signal and they cannot afford to turn a deaf ear to what they are feeling at this time.

I am here for all of My children and I will protect them. They do not need to live their lives as victims any longer. Please remind all of My children of My promised kingdom to come. There are so many now who are learning at a rapid rate. **Use these circumstances which you are witnessing to fine tune your appreciation of that**

which truly matters! Do not spend time now on that which does not nurture your soul.

Talk then to My people about the power of prayer! For I hear all of your prayers as My heart is heavy for those who are suffering. I will do all within My power to save as many souls as possible. Yet, you must understand the importance of this battle now and look to that which is the reality. Do not be deceived or lulled into submission. You cannot afford to turn a deaf ear for it is this deaf ear that Satan has counted on for much of his success. I am giving you all the keys now to help you negate that which is to come. **You have all that you need within you. You must now be the leaders of the future.** *It is your turn to serve and I ask you to use everything, every message at your disposal. Do not be soldiers of fear that is what Satan counts on.* **I ask you now to be soldiers of light girded with armors of hope.** *Show My people a new way of life. For now many will be open to that which is of the Divine.*

I want My children to think about the people who play an integral part in each of their lives. Think of those you trust and then think on those who you do not have the same level of trust for. You will begin to clearly see those who are of like minds. These are the people you should interact with. These are the people who will respond to what they hear from Me. They will know that which they are called to do and understand the role they will now play. They will understand the importance of these times and act upon that which they hear when they go to the cave within.

*Those you love will be watching your actions at this time. You must be messengers of hope and light. Let others see your inner strength and calm reserve. There will be many who will need to see this now. Therefore, watch your actions and come to Me when you are in doubt as to what to say or do. This is not training time now; this is the time to do that which you have learned from Me. Keep your eyes, hearts, and minds on that which is of the Divine. Keep your feet firmly planted now in My kingdom, not that which is of this world. Do those activities of a joyful nature not that of a temporal nature. Do everything in your power to exercise that of the spirit, that which is of My kingdom. Stay away from darkness and look into the light. When you are in the creative plain it is far easier to partake of the light than when you are in the confines of your mind. Even those who are working can now spend more time with Me as they focus on that which is of My kingdom. **Right mind set brings about right action**. Your lives are so very precious as are the lives of those you love. Please, all of you, use your time wisely. Help others to see how important this is to live in the moment. How important it is to listen to that which comes from the center of their being. Man cannot afford to be complacent any longer. **When all things come together in the name of the Father many great works will be accomplished**. You must **show** them how to do this! I see your faithfulness now little ones, simply do as I ask and you will be responding to My call! **Encourage all then to use their gifts for the betterment of mankind!**"*

Chapter 9

Conclusion from Wendy and Jillian

Wendy and Jillian knew time was of the utmost importance. There would be so many *earth angels* who needed to hear what their beloved Jesus had to say. There would be many, like the two of them, who now fully understood the significance of the times. Although there were many *earth angels* who knew what their true purpose was they would come to understand much more upon reading the book, for Jesus was giving them the tools that would help each of them accomplish their missions.

Wendy had done her very best to insure she had written the messages precisely as Jesus intended. She knew how much was at stake for all and could not afford to misrepresent any part of what Jesus had asked her to write. She had faith that if there was something that needed changing or something else to be included He would let her know when in communion with Him.

These are the times now that mankind must come together in numbers to drive Satan and his army from this earth. Although, it will indeed be the greatest battle of all times, Jesus has formed a covenant with His chosen that cannot be broken. There is a new world coming for all who believe!

However you have come to read this book you must know it is not a coincidence but intended for you at this time. You must believe the answers you seek will now come from within. You will see through this communion what has always been there for all to avail oneself of. This is so important in the days and weeks to come as the adversary will do all in his power to promote fear. He will do all in his power to keep God's kingdom from coming to pass on this earth. Satan will use tools of doubt, skepticism and financial unrest to keep all from fulfilling their higher purpose.

It is the Father's fervent desire that as many souls as possible will be saved. Each of us must now be willing to listen to what our Father has to say to His children. You will find the answers you seek when you go to the cave within. You can be confident you will find Him there ready and willing to converse with each of you.

You must now transition yourself from those things and thoughts of the world knowing He is there for each and every one of His children anytime day or night. Jesus is the reality! He and His kingdom are not the illusion. In the end it will be His kingdom that does indeed reign on this earth. We are here to help with this transition. We are here to come together in these days with our gifts and talents to make a new world for all of mankind. You can be confident this is His **Great Plan**! In truth this is the greatest plan of all.

For evil will be overthrown. Satan and his army will finally be banned from this earth for many years to come. Therefore, do not be frightened. He will send what each of us needs at precisely the right time. He only asks now that we proceed with confidence. He asks we open up our hearts to those around us sharing all that we know with others. Do not be humble in our Father's regard! We are His soldiers on earth. You know what your gift is. What He asks now is that each of us uses our gifts, as they were intended from the very beginning.

Personal Note from the Authors:

Jillian and I understand there will be those who read this book who may or may not choose to share their gifts with others. But know this! You would not have been given these gifts if our Holy Father did not want you to share them with all. You now understand how important each of our gifts are to one another.

You have always had our Father at your disposal 24 hours a day. He has always been there waiting for you to have a *conversation* with Him. Satan has deceived many for such a long time and now you will see how closely connected each of us is to the Divine!

We do not need to live by the standards of man any longer! We need to seek higher standards now. We need to listen to what the Spirit is calling each of us to do and move forward with confidence. We all will be infused with a new **enthusiasm** as we proceed forward with that which we are called to do!

Remember "**The secret to living is in the giving!**"

ABBA and Company

ABBA and Company was founded in 1995 by Gwen Michalek and Jill Emerson. ABBA offers classes in "The Art of Joy-filled Living". Our primary objective is to help individuals identify and develop their own special and unique God given gifts and talents. When individuals are in touch with their natural gifts and talents they experience a true and lasting Joy in all areas of their lives and are able to make a positive difference in our world today.

We offer our services to any individual, company, or organization that shares in this commitment to improving the lives of all people.

ABBA and Company Mission Statement

ABBA and Company has been founded as a result of its supreme commitment to the betterment of mankind. The primary objective is to teach others to maximize their potential for the good of self and others. ABBA and Company believes that all individuals are created with an inherent gift which when nurtured and encouraged will provide a significant contribution towards the improvement of mankind.

For more information on ABBA and Company and to purchase our books visit:

www.earthangelsbook.com

Preview of Book 2

"Well" exclaimed the Angel of Joy, "This is indeed is a day for much celebration! I knew Wendy and Jillian would succeed, St. Michael. I told you to stop worrying. You can see for yourself they made it to the beach to finish writing the book without a scratch. True, they got a little carried away that first night but that's to be expected! After all, it isn't as though they get away together all that often. Anyway, I thought it was cute

how the more they analyzed what Jesus meant about practicing tolerance, the more wine they drank. Goes to show you we all must be tolerant of one another at times including our own behaviors, as well, be it on earth or in heaven!

"Yes," responded St. Michael. "I was most anxious their trip might be delayed once again. I should have realized Jesus would not allow anything to stand in their way now. I know how anxious you and the others have been regarding their safety. I know how diligent you are my friend and that you would see to it no mortal harm would come to them in these days. Thank you my dear Joy! I am most anxious for my two *earth angels* now. I am certain Satan knows how important the work they are doing is and yes, I know Jesus has formed a covenant with each of them. I also know, as well as you, what a formidable foe the adversary is. I am well aware of the subtle way he operates. He will prey on their individual weaknesses, of that you can be certain. I feel so helpless when I can see they are under attack. While I can keep them from physical harm I cannot keep them from the myriad of emotions he can invoke. I can see they now are well versed in the tools Satan uses. For awhile there I truly thought they were done in. I should have realized Jesus' timing was the key. Even I thought they were dangerously close to abandoning their mission. It must have been very nerve wracking for you, as their mentor!"

"Well yes," Joy responded, "I have been anxious more than a few times, I must admit. Yet, I had faith they would continue to be filled with Divine inspiration. You know how persistent our Father can be, not to mention there have been so many in the heavens praying for them on a daily basis. Why there are those in the heavens who, having known them personally on earth, follow their activities quite regularly. Just the other day I heard one of them comment on how proud they were to have been a part of their lives. Yes, there are many now watching as Wendy and Jillian proceed with their mission."

There is such a massive movement taking place. If only the *earth angels* could see what we in the heavens can see. If only they knew how many of them now were scattered around the world. They would be most amazed indeed. I know Wendy and Jillian are most anxious to join forces with the others. It must seem as though it has taken such a long time for this moment to come. There has been so much advance preparation and now that the time has come, much will be accomplished in such a short time.

Jillian is working hard to compile and edit the final draft of the book and soon it will be passed along for publishing. I will see to it each gets the time to complete their part. They are infused now with the Holy Spirit and will pay close attention to what they are called to do, on a daily basis. Why even now Wendy is responding to Divine inspiration. She has already started the second book!"

"The second book! Are you serious?" questioned St. Michael, "The first one hasn't even been published yet. What on earth is she thinking? I already am having a challenge keeping Satan at bay. This will surely provoke him.

"Whoops, I have to go, looks like Wendy is in danger on her way home from the beach!" cried St Michael, "seems there is someone who is trying to run her and her husband Dick off the road. I need to make certain Dick keeps a cool head. He doesn't realize who he is dealing with. See, I told you Satan was on to them. Be back in a flash!"

Wendy could not believe this was happening. Where on earth did this car come from and why was he trying to pass them when the passing lane was ending. Wendy had been lost in her own thoughts and was drawn to abrupt attention when she heard the horn honk from behind. Dick slowed down as the passing lane ended. He could see a truck coming ...